Dem Little Bums:
The Nashua Dodgers

Dem Little Bums:
The Nashua Dodgers

the story of their vital role in the
racial integration of baseball,
and of their rapid fall from grace,
1946–1949

by Steve Daly

PLAIDSWEDE PUBLISHING
Concord, New Hampshire

ISBN 0-9626832-4-8
Library of Congress Control Number: 2002106506

Designed and composed in Electra at Hobblebush Books,
Brookline, New Hampshire (www.hobblebush.com)

Printed in the United States of America

Published by:

PLAIDSWEDE PUBLISHING
P.O. BOX 269 · CONCORD, NEW HAMPSHIRE 03302-0269
www.plaidswede.com

*To my Dad, the biggest baseball fan
I know and the best father
anyone could hope for*

Acknowledgments

THIS BOOK WOULD NOT have been possible without the help and input of many people. Some were subtle in their influence; others had more of a role in the completion of this project than they could ever imagine.

Of course, none of this could have been possible without the help of the many former players and baseball executives who offered their memories and recollections. There are too many to name, but the contributions of Don Newcombe, Bill Eberly, Buzzie Bavasi, Bob Kehoe and Pete Giordano were essential.

The editing help of John Enright, Tom Auclair, Cindy Cloutier and Alan Greenwood helped tie up some loose ends and make the story more presentable. The photography work of Don Himsel and Pete Carvelli helped allow the pictures to offer more insight into the players and their stories.

The input of Ted Fay and David Ryan helped provide direction in the early going, while the guidance and experience of George Geers and Sid Hall helped mold the final product.

Finally, the patience, enthusiasm and encouragement from my family helped make this a labor of love. To my wife, Maureen, and daughters, Brooke and Katherine, a heartfelt thank you.

—Steve Daly

FROM THE NASHUA DODGERS TO THE NASHUA PRIDE, *The Telegraph* has reported the baseball story at historic Holman Stadium to the readers of greater Nashua. This book by a member of the paper's sports staff is continued proof of the paper's commitment to baseball in Nashua. The publisher gratefully acknowledges the support of *The Telegraph* in publishing *Dem Little Bums: The Nashua Dodgers*.

— George L. Geers, Publisher, Plaidswede Publishing Co.

Contents

Foreword

THE CITY OF NASHUA should be held in high regard for what it did to help integrate the great game of baseball.

I had just been discharged from the service after spending three years in the African and Italian campaigns as an infantryman during World War II. On my discharge, my wife and I and our young son had leased a home in Sea Island, Ga., with the intent to take a year off before joining the Dodgers.

However, Mr. Rickey summoned me to New York and asked if I would operate a club in the New England League for one year. He was having difficulty finding a city for Roy Campanella and Don Newcombe to play in. Kish Bookwalter, owner of the Danville, Ill., club did not think his city was ready for such an adventure. I was then asked to find a city where the young men would be welcome.

After talking to *The Nashua Telegraph's* managing editor, Fred Dobens, I knew that Nashua was the place. Thus came the Nashua Dodgers.

The Dodgers had over 20 minor league clubs at the time, but the Dodgers did not want Newk or Campy to start in a high classification. But all the lower classifications were in towns like Pine Bluff, Paducah, Hazzard, Daytona Beach—mostly in the deep South.

The choice of Nashua turned out to be perfect. The citizens of Nashua fell in love with Newk and Campy, and they in turn loved playing there.

I'd have to say that Fred Dobens made it all possible.

E.J. "Buzzie" Bavasi
Nashua Dodgers Business Manager (1946)
Jan. 7, 2000

Introduction

Don Newcombe kicked at the loose dirt around the pitching rubber and cast his eyes toward the catcher. He rolled back on his heels, lifted his left leg and pulled his right hand—with a gleaming white baseball gripped tightly across the wide seams—away from his left. His head turned slightly left, his bespectacled eyes searched for the catcher's leather mitt and honed in on the grimy pocket.

A former teammate once said Don Newcombe could throw a baseball so hard that it could travel through a shower room without getting wet, but today he was more concerned with accuracy than speed. The 70-year-old's pitch tailed off the plate, nearly into the dirt, but the young catcher side-stepped to catch it and cupped his right hand across the pocket to prevent the ball from dropping out.

The crowd erupted.

Don Newcombe took off his cap and acknowledged the applause. After a 50-year odyssey, when his right arm made him a baseball hero from Brooklyn to Los Angeles to Japan, and later, when his drive and determination helped him overcome an alcohol addiction, Don Newcombe was back home. Back where it all began, in Nashua, New Hampshire.

To his side on this glorious spring afternoon in 1997 was Roy Campanella's widow, Roxie, spending her first day in a city in which her late husband and his best friend became cult heroes.

In 1946, Don Newcombe and Roy Campanella had joined Jackie Robinson in breaking the color barrier, becoming the first African-Americans to play for an affiliated baseball team in the United States since left-handed pitcher Jimmy Claxton appeared in both games of a doubleheader on May 28, 1916, during a six-day career with the Oakland Oaks of the Pacific Coast League. Before that, no black had played in organized "white" baseball since Moses Fleetwood Walker caught 42 games for the Toledo Blue Stockings of the American Association in 1884. His brother, Welday, played five games as an outfielder on that same team.

But Cap Anson, widely recognized as an ambassador of the game who improved the quality of play in the fledgling sport and organized a world tour in 1888–89, was also considered an unwavering bigot. A powerful manager and part-owner of the Chicago White Stockings, Anson pulled his team off the field rather than play against a team that had a black player. In 1884, he helped forge a "gentlemen's agreement," an unwritten rule that prevented blacks from playing in affiliated baseball until Robinson made his debut with the Montreal Royals of the International League on April 18, 1946, and 20 days before Newcombe and Campanella took the field for the Nashua Dodgers.

Newcombe and Campanella kept in constant touch with Robinson. Late-night telephone calls between Campanella and Robinson kept the players updated on each other's progress as well as their adaptations to their new surroundings.

The French-Canadians embraced Robinson from the beginning. He and his wife Rachel became a part of the community, as well as a symbol of perseverance. Most of their problems came when the Montreal Royals were on the road. Robinson was blistered with racial epithets and degrading insults when the team played in Baltimore and Syracuse. But Robinson, as much as he wanted to fight back, absorbed the punishment. There were bigger fights ahead.

Brooklyn Dodgers president Branch Rickey was determined to do everything in his power to integrate baseball. In Jackie Robinson, he chose the right man. Robinson was as determined as Rickey to erase 62 years of bigotry. Jackie Robinson was to be the first African-American in "white" baseball.

In Nashua, Newcombe and Campanella received much the same community and team support as Robinson in Montreal. Newcombe, a 19-year-old right-handed pitcher from Elizabeth, N.J., was one of the hardest throwers in the New England League. He also had a bit of a temper. Campanella was his foil. A 25-year-old catcher from Philadelphia and the son of an Italian immigrant and a black woman, Campanella was as gentle as he was talented.

"By the end of that 1946 season, either one of those guys could have run for mayor and won easily," said E.J. "Buzzie" Bavasi, the Nashua Dodgers' business manager.

In 1997, Newcombe was being treated like the mayor. Returning to Holman Stadium for a ceremony recognizing his and Campanella's contributions to the integration of baseball, he was also back home after 50 years.

Newcombe spied a familiar face at the edge of the crowd. "Roomie!" he shouted as he hurried over to embrace Gus Galipeau, the Nashua Dodgers' backup catcher in 1946 and '47, and Newcombe's roommate during their second season together. The two clung to each other, long-lost brothers.

While Newcombe and Campanella went on to successful major league careers, Galipeau became the player-manager of St. Hyacinthe, Quebec, in 1948 in the semi-professional Provincial League, a circuit of textile industry teams. He continued his off-season career as a defenseman in professional hockey before giving up baseball and hockey and beginning a career as a police officer on the Woonsocket (R.I.) Police Department, a job he held for 32 years.

As the Dodgers checked into their hotel in Portland, Maine, on their first road trip of the 1947 season, both Galipeau and Newcombe found themselves without roommates. Galipeau, figuring they were a pretty good match as battery-mates, thought they could survive as roommates.

"We're standing in the lobby of the hotel in Portland and I said, 'Don, who you rooming with?'" Galipeau remembered.

"No one, Gus," Newcombe replied.

"'Sign your name and pick up your bags. We're roommates,'" Galipeau said.

With that, Galipeau and Newcombe became the first interracial roommates in professional baseball.

All that seemed so long ago. As Newcombe basked in the bright sunshine and adulation of the crowd at Holman Stadium, Galipeau stood quietly to the side, content to let his friend and roommate get all the attention he deserved.

The glory days of baseball had returned to Nashua and historic Holman Stadium, if only for one day.

Dem Little Bums:
The Nashua Dodgers

A League is (Re)born

CLAUDE B. DAVIDSON'S CAREER statistics in the major leagues pale in comparison to thousands of names in the Baseball Encyclopedia. A 5-foot-11, 155-pound infielder from Boston, Davidson played in 31 games with the Philadelphia Athletics in 1918, including 15 at second base, batting just .185 with a double and four runs batted in. He was 2-for-7 as a pinch hitter on a Connie Mack-managed team that went 52–76 and finished dead last in the American League.

In 1919, after playing for New Haven in the Eastern League, Davidson appeared in two games at third base with the Washington Senators, going 3-for-7 filling in for Eddie "Kid" Foster, the Senators' aptly nicknamed (5-foot-6½, 145 pounds) regular third baseman. A "poisoned foot" suffered in his second game with the Senators forced Davidson to return to his Dorchester, Mass., home to recuperate.

He was out of organized baseball soon after and began coaching at Harvard University, where he was the freshman coach in 1925. He managed to find time for himself on the field, as well, becoming president and founder of the semi-professional Boston Twilight League while also playing third base for the Dorchester team.

Davidson always extolled the virtues of professional baseball in New England beyond the major league Red Sox and Braves. The Class B New England League dated back to 1884, but financial woes and other problems had haunted the league at nearly every turn. Riding on the coattails of an Allied victory in World War I, John H. Donnelly attempted to resurrect the New England League in 1919, but after the Lowell and Lawrence, Mass., teams disbanded on July 15, the entire league shut down Aug. 2.

Davidson had hoped things would be different when he assumed the presidency of the NEL in 1926, and he got his wish. There was a remarkable rise in the popularity of baseball after World War I. At its height in the Roaring Twenties, the National Association had nearly 30 leagues in operation, from AA-level franchises in the American and International leagues, down to tiny Class D outposts in the Oklahoma State and Kitty leagues.

The New England League was no exception. Reborn in 1926, with teams in eight cities in Massachusetts, New Hampshire and Maine, the New England League spawned such players as catcher Shanty Hogan, who after two years in which he played in just 13 games with the Boston Red Sox, tore up the NEL with Lynn, Mass., in 1926, leading the circuit in home runs (19) and runs batted in (89) in 95 games. He went on to play 976 more games and hit .295 in 11 major league seasons with the Red Sox, New York Yankees, Boston Braves and Washington Senators.

Hogan's teammate, King Lore Bader, who had pitched with the New York Giants (1912) and Red Sox (1917–18), led the New England League with a 2.64 ERA. Jay J. O'Connor of the Haverhill, Mass., team led the league in batting at .394.

Baseball was alive and well in the mill towns of New England.

The league flourished for three seasons before history interfered with the Great Depression in 1929. Neither the Lowell nor Haverhill franchises survived the summer of 1929; Lowell moved its operations to Nashua on June 20 and Haverhill fled to Fitchburg, Mass., on July 24, then to Gloucester, Mass., on Aug. 20. It was no coincidence that the teams were the worst two in the New England League.

The NEL was one of 23 leagues to begin the 1930 season — and one of two to disband during the summer. Nashua, which had only regained a franchise when the Lowell team moved north the previous season, again couldn't support the team and joined Lewiston, Maine, in dropping out of the league on June 15. One week later, the remaining teams in Salem and Lynn, Mass., Manchester, N.H., and Portland, Maine, disbanded.

The New England League resurfaced in 1933, but instability again was the rule of thumb. New Bedford held off Worcester to win the regular-season title with a 58–33 record, then refused to take part in a playoff system because it felt it had already won the championship. Second-place Worcester (54–33) instead faced third-place Lowell (49–40) and split the first two games of the best-of-five series. Rain unceremoniously washed out the remaining games of the championship series in September, and, as it turned out, the final days of the New England League.

During that final season, the Attleboro, Mass., franchise was uprooted after less than a month, moving first to Lawrence, Mass., and then Woonsocket, R.I. The Quincy,

Mass., franchise moved to Nashua on June 5 and stayed until Aug. 10 when it packed up and left for Brockton, Mass. Once again, the two teams with the worst records in the league played the roles of nomads.

Claude Davidson's vision of a return of minor league baseball to New England had vaporized. It would be another 13 years before a refurbished NEL would reappear, again on the heels of another defining moment—the surrender of the Japanese after the atomic bombing of Hiroshima and Nagasaki in 1945, marking the end of World War II.

◆ ◆ ◆ ◆

As early as the first few days of 1946, word spread that the New England League would resurface as an eight-team circuit. On January 14, it became official: The season would open in the first week of May with a 126-game schedule running through Labor Day, with Sunday and evening games planned.

Representatives from Lynn and Fall River in Massachusetts, Nashua and Manchester in New Hampshire, Providence, R.I., and Portland, Maine, met with Claude Davidson in a Boston social club, and Davidson was named league president and secretary. Each of the six clubs posted the required $1,500 bond for entry in the league. A week later, Pawtucket, R.I., and Lawrence, Mass., were accepted into the league.

The Boston Red Sox immediately announced an affiliation with Lynn and named Thomas "Pip" Kennedy as manager. The Nashua franchise would be owned outright by the Brooklyn Dodgers, and E.J. "Buzzie" Bavasi, a rising executive in the club's Ebbets Field offices, was named general manager.

Rumors were rampant that Stanley "Frenchy" Bordagaray would be named manager of the Nashua Dodgers, a natural for the city's bastion of French-Canadians. Bordagaray was an 11-year veteran of the major leagues, having spent the final four years of his career with Brooklyn, and hit .256 in 113 games as an outfielder with the Dodgers in 1945. But local club representatives insisted that the team's manager not be named until the end of spring training.

On March 13, 1946, Nashua officially announced the Dodgers would call Holman Stadium home, ending weeks of haggling over the amount of money the city would receive in rent payments. The return of pro ball to Nashua was expected to boost interest in the game and improve what once was considered one of the best diamonds in New England.

Bavasi wasn't tipping his hand at naming a manager, but promised that the selection would be announced within a week and that the skipper would most likely be a player-manager. At nine-year-old Holman Stadium, constructed as part of a WPA project in 1937, lights were erected to provide the first night baseball games in city history.

Meanwhile, the guardians of white professional baseball had been dealt a shocking blow. In October 1945, Jackie Robinson, a 27-year-old shortstop with the Kansas City Monarchs of the Negro Leagues, was signed by Brooklyn. Branch Rickey was beginning his quest to shatter baseball's racial barrier. At the forefront of the signing was Clyde Sukeforth, the team's 45-year-old chief scout and a former catcher with the Cincinnati Reds and Dodgers. Sukeforth had spent the summer of 1926 in Nashua, where he batted .367 as a rookie with the Nashua Millionaires of the old New England League. He made his major league debut that same summer, playing one game with the Reds.

Sukeforth had quietly followed Rickey's instructions to

find a talented ballplayer, but, more importantly, one who could withstand the strain of being the first African-American to play in organized white baseball since the early part of the century. And Robinson would merely be the start; Rickey planned to bring more African-American ballplayers to follow Robinson.

After months of trailing Robinson, traveling by train through the night to catch Monarchs games all over the eastern half of the United States, Sukeforth realized he had found the ballplayer Rickey had sought. Jackie Robinson was one of the nation's greatest collegiate athletes while at the University of California at Los Angeles. His mother had packed him, his brothers and sisters onto a train under cover of the Georgia night and headed to Pasadena, Calif., to escape the racial turbulence of the Deep South. A former lieutenant in the U.S. Army who had survived a court-martial and eventual acquittal while stationed in Texas because he refused to move to the back of the bus, Robinson had a unique combination of talent, competitive fire, poise, maturity and intelligence. He would need every one of those attributes in the months and years ahead.

Rickey's selection of Robinson was the beginning. In the spring of 1946, Rickey had heard of a promising second baseman playing for the Negro Leagues' Newark Eagles across the Upper New York Bay in New Jersey. He was intrigued enough to call on one of his better judges of talent.

"Whenever Mr. Rickey needed someone in a hurry, they always called for me," Sukeforth said. "I ran into him one night down at the offices and he asked me to take a run over to see Mrs. (Effa) Manley's club. He told me to pay attention to the second baseman.

"So I headed over there and saw the second baseman, and he was a fine athlete and a good prospect. But when the game started, out trotted this 19-year-old colored kid who threw harder than anyone (the Dodgers) had ever had.

"The next day, Mr. Rickey said, 'Did you see that second baseman last night?' I kind of hesitated, and Mr. Rickey asked if I had gone over there. I said, 'Mr. Rickey, that second baseman is a good ballplayer, but I saw this pitcher . . .'"

" 'Did you get his name?' Mr. Rickey asked. I smiled and said, 'I sure did.' "

At 6-foot-4 and possessing a windup that had batters wondering where the ball was coming from, Don Newcombe was an intimidating presence on the pitcher's mound. He was also unafraid to let batters know he intended to control the strike zone — throwing the ball wherever he had to to establish his territory.

Newcombe's arrival in the Negro Leagues was at the end of an odd trip. As a youngster, he envisioned a career as a long-distance truck driver; at 16, Newcombe took a job with a New Jersey trucking company and his first assignment was to make a delivery to Memphis, Tenn. Problem was, once Newcombe made the delivery, he had no way of getting back to New Jersey because the vehicle was not scheduled to return.

Around the same time, Newcombe made the equally unwise decision to join the U.S. Army, meeting with a recruiter and signing all the necessary paperwork after lying about his age. But while Newcombe was in Tennessee trying to find a way to get home, he had missed his reporting date. The Army, figuring Newcombe was reneging on his decision to enlist, considered him AWOL and issued a warrant for his arrest.

Newcombe's father, meanwhile, desperately tried to convince the government that Newcombe wasn't even eligible to enlist, having been months shy of his 18th birthday and, thus, legally unable to make the decision to join. Finally, after the senior Newcombe was able to produce a birth certificate to prove his son's age, the agreement was nullified.

After high school, Newcombe spent two seasons pitching for the Newark Eagles under manager Mule Suttles, winning one game and losing two in four appearances in 1944, walking eight and giving up 29 hits in just 18 innings while striking out eight. But in his second season, in 1945—and still just 18 years old when the season started—Newcombe blossomed, winning six games and losing two, striking out 23 in 70 innings while giving up just 48 hits and three walks. He completed six of the seven games he started.

His numbers were impressive, seeing he often found himself pitching against some of the Negro League's most storied players: Cool Papa Bell and Josh Gibson of the Homestead Grays; Martin Dihigo of the New York Cubans; and a stocky catcher for the Baltimore Elite Giants named Roy Campanella.

Rickey told Sukeforth to bring Newcombe into the team offices on Montague Street in Brooklyn on a Saturday, an unusual day, Sukeforth remembers, because the offices weren't often open then. Newcombe arrived and waited outside Rickey's office. After about two hours and obviously feeling he was wasting his time, Newcombe stood to leave but Sukeforth stopped him. The scout barged into Rickey's office as he was conducting an organizational meeting and apprised him of the situation. Rickey, still having not met or talked to Newcombe, instructed Sukeforth to sign the young pitcher. Newcombe walked out as the newest player of the Brooklyn Dodgers organization.

In 1945, the 23-year-old Campanella, the son of an Italian father and black mother from Philadelphia, was already in his eighth season of professional baseball, having joined the Elite Giants when he was 16 years old. But Campanella had been getting paid to play baseball since he was 15, earning $35 a week to play two games on weekends for the Bacharach Giants, a prominent Negro semi-pro team from Philadelphia.

At 5 feet, 9½ inches and 190 pounds, Campanella had established himself as one of the best catchers in the Negro Leagues. He became the Elite Giants' starting catcher in his second season and led the team to wins over the Newark Eagles and Homestead Grays in the playoffs. Beginning in 1940 he would hit over .300 in six straight seasons, also leading the Negro Leagues in runs batted in in 1945.

But he knew he could do more.

Campanella and Newcombe joined some of the Negro Leagues' best players in a series of games in October 1945 against a collection of major leaguers coached by Brooklyn manager Charlie Dressen. After the third game of the series at Newark's Ruppert Stadium, Dressen approached Campanella and told him that Rickey would like to speak with him the next morning.

Rickey was interested in adding Campanella to his growing list of potential ground-breakers and asked him if he'd like to join the Dodgers organization. But Campanella was unaware that Rickey had envisioned Campanella one day crouching behind the plate for the Brooklyn Dodgers. Campanella had assumed Rickey was interested in placing him on the Brooklyn Brown Dodgers, a team that was to play in a new Negro league Rickey was contemplating beginning. After nine years in the Negro Leagues and becoming one of the league's best-paid players, though, Campanella wasn't interested in starting all over again in a new league. He declined Rickey's invitation, but promised not to sign with another team before first telling the Dodgers.

In the fall, before embarking on a barnstorming trip to South America, Campanella and Robinson were talking in the Woodside Hotel in Harlem. Robinson had known that Campanella had met with Rickey and asked him how it went. When Campanella told Robinson that he had decided against accepting Rickey's offer, Robinson asked Campanella if Rickey had asked him to play for the Brown Dodgers. Campanella realized that Rickey had never actually named the team. When Robinson told Campanella that it would soon be announced that he had signed a contract to play for the Montreal Royals, the Dodgers' top farm club in the International League, Campanella feared that he had blown his chance to play in the major leagues.

After sending word to Rickey that he had reconsidered joining the Dodgers organization, Campanella headed to South America, unsure he would get a second chance. Finally, on March 1, 1946, after a long, anxious winter, Campanella got a telegram from Rickey telling him to report to Brooklyn on March 10. The only problem was the owner of Campanella's team in Venezuela didn't want him to leave because Campanella was the team's only catcher. He relented, though, when the team's center fielder, Sam Jethroe, volunteered to catch. Campanella caught a flight that day for New York.

Upon arriving in New York, Campanella was told that Rickey was in Sanford, Fla., observing Robinson's first spring training with the Dodgers. But there was trouble. Civic leaders in Florida were unhappy with the presence of a black ballplayer and some teams were refusing to honor their commitments to spring exhibition games. Suddenly, Campanella's dreams of joining Robinson in Florida and being a teammate of his in Montreal were imperiled.

Bob Finch, Rickey's assistant, signed Campanella to a player contract and called representatives of the Class B Danville (Ill.) Dodgers, where Campanella was expected to make his debut in organized ball. But before Finch hung up the phone, Campanella knew those plans had fallen through as well.

Tom Fairweather, the president of the Three-I League, of which Danville was a member, refused to allow its teams to field black players.

"If you send them here," he reportedly said, "I'll disband the league."

After more calls to different farm clubs were answered with apprehension and outright refusal, Rickey urged Finch to call Buzzie Bavasi in Nashua.

Campanella was tiring of the runaround. "They were tossing me from team to team with nobody wanting anything to do with me," Campanella wrote in his 1959 autobiography, *It's Good to be Alive*. "They were playing catch with my career and all I could do was listen. First I was bitter, then I became angry.

"I decided I should have known better than to even hope this white man's league would want any part of fellows like me. They were already beginning to get on Jackie. Maybe I was better off to have never even gotten started."

But Finch got the answer he needed from Bavasi.

Campanella thought he heard Finch say he'd be playing in "Nashville." Knowing the racial climate in that Tennessee city, Campanella was leery.

"No, Nashua," Finch replied. "It's in New Hampshire, also Class B. They've got a new general manager up there, fellow named Buzzie Bavasi. Buzzie is one of the finest young fellows in the organization. He's smart and progressive. You'll like him."

The plans were complete. Finch told Campanella he would arrange for his railroad ticket to Nashua and some expense money. What Campanella didn't realize was that he wouldn't be making his journey north to New Hampshire by himself.

"Oh, by the way, you're going to have company on your train ride to Nashua," Finch said as Campanella reached for the door. "A young Negro pitcher named Don Newcombe."

◆ ◆ ◆ ◆

As their future teammates were hundreds of miles away in Thomasville, N.C., finishing spring training workouts that kicked off the return of professional baseball to Nashua for the first time in more than 13 years, Newcombe and Campanella sat in their cabin at a local motel, wondering what the future might hold.

In a few days, they would make history by becoming the first two black ballplayers to play for a major league-affiliated team in the United States in the modern era. Days earlier, Jackie Robinson had made his professional debut in Montreal.

"Are we doing the right thing?" Newcombe asked Campanella.

Campanella, in his usual self-assured manner, told him they were.

"Everything will be all right," Campanella told him. "You'll see."

"(Robinson) and Campy had distinctively different temperaments and approaches to dealing with white people,"

Rachel Robinson, Jackie's wife, wrote in her poignant memoir, *Jackie Robinson: An Intimate Portrait.* "Jack was reserved and direct at the same time, impatient for signs of progress, and unwilling to accept affronts to his dignity or challenges to the rights of others. Some sportswriters described his forcefulness as 'black rage' and said he had 'a chip on his shoulder.' . . . Assertive black men were viewed as 'aggressive,' prone to violence, and threatening—a widely held stereotype even today.

"Campy's style and attitude made him more accepted. He was gentler and more accommodating, less apt to challenge. He was described as 'likable.' Although he and Jack were pushed by the press to disavow each other—and occasionally they succumbed—they remained lifelong friends."

The African-American ballplayers were used to rejection. No black man had appeared in the major leagues since Moses Fleetwood Walker, who played 42 games for the Toledo Blue Stockings in 1884. Jimmy Claxton, whose fair complexion enabled him to pitch in two games for the minor-league Oakland Oaks in 1916 before he too was expelled, was the last black to appear in a organized baseball.

Branch Rickey was tearing down the wall. He started with the Montreal Royals; the next step was the Nashua Dodgers.

"Don't worry," Campanella said again. "We'll be OK."

*Don Newcombe, in 1946, the first of his two
seasons with the Nashua Dodgers.*

1946:
Breaking Down Barriers

CLAUDE B. DAVIDSON'S DREAM of a reformed New England League—with Nashua as a cornerstone franchise—began to take shape in the first days of 1946, nearly 13 years after the Nashua Millionaires recorded the last out of their final NEL season in 1933. But as soon as a week before the league was made official, stories about Nashua's landing a Brooklyn Dodgers farm club had appeared in *The Nashua Telegraph*.

Rickey chose Bavasi to take the reins of the Nashua franchise, and Walter Alston, a former first baseman who struck out in his only major-league at-bat in 1936 with the St. Louis Cardinals, was named player/manager of the Dodgers. He had decided to take a leave of absence from his teaching and coaching position at Lewiston (Ohio) High School to stay in baseball, at least for another summer.

Both Bavasi and Alston were interested in doing anything they could to improve the ballclub. When Finch, on orders from Rickey, pitched the idea of Newcombe and Campanella starting their careers in Nashua, Bavasi had only one concern.

"As long as they can play baseball, it's all right with me," Bavasi told Finch.

◆ ◆ ◆ ◆

The story trumpeting the signings of Campanella and Newcombe to contracts with the Nashua Dodgers was buried on Page 19 of the April 4, 1946, edition of *The Nashua Telegraph*. On a day when readers learned that Russia had agreed to pull its troops out of Iran, tidal waves had caused $10 million in damage in Hawaii, and Edmond Dugas, one of four Nashua brothers to serve his country in World War II, would be returning to his hometown to a hero's welcome, one of the most important social steps of the 20th century was delegated to the first sports page.

> *Branch Rickey of the Brooklyn Dodgers will test New England fandom's democratic attitude toward the racial question this spring, it was revealed today, with the announcement that the Brooklyn baseball club has signed two more Negro players and will place them with their New England League farm team here in Nashua.*
>
> *Signed to Nashua contracts by the Brooklyn management are Donald Newcombe, right-handed pitcher from Elizabeth, N.J., and Roy Campanella, a catcher from Philadelphia. Both will report to Nashua for the opening of preseason drills at Holman Stadium, April 18.*

Newcombe was "regarded by Dodgers scouts ... as the best of the young colored hurlers in the strong Negro loop," the story stated. As for Campanella, he was "immediately tabbed by far the outstanding candidate for the major leagues to be found in Negro baseball circles." Even better, apparently, than Jackie Robinson.

An indication of the newspaper's reasons for relegating the story to the sports section may have been revealed later in the article.

> *For Nashua baseball fans, watching Negro ballplayers in action will be no innovation. The local fans have watched such Negro clubs as the New York Colored Giants perform here, and have liked them. However, fans will watch for the first time Negro players in action with white players in organized ball.*

Several days later, however, managing editor Fred Dobens, in one of his daily editorials, acknowledged that Campanella and Newcombe wouldn't have the benefit of being treated like any other ballplayer on the first-year Dodgers team.

> *Nashua's baseball entry in the New England League is making an experiment in better race relations by giving Negro players a chance to make good in organized ball.*
>
> *The parent team, the Brooklyn Dodgers of the National League, is sending two Negroes to the city to try out for the Nashua team. According to reports, they are outstanding players. Unfortunately, they will have to be to make good even in the kind of organized baseball played here.*
>
> *A Negro must stand head and shoulders above other competitors to win a place for himself these days. The same will be true for the two who come here.*

Dobens' role in helping pave the way for the Dodgers' arrival—and more specifically a smooth transition for Campanella and Newcombe—is one that has never been truly appreciated. As the primary voice of the local newspaper, Dobens yielded a tremendous amount of clout and power, more so than even some of the local politicos. He was the eyes and ears of Nashua—what was good for the city was also good for the newspaper.

In 1946, Nashua was roughly one-third the size it is today, but *The Nashua Telegraph* had virtual saturation coverage of the city's homes. As former publisher Albert Spendlove said, everybody knew everyone else, and you can be sure that everyone knew Fred Dobens.

A lifelong Nashua resident and unfailing supporter of the Gate City, Dobens surely knew a remarkable opportunity when he saw it. Brooklyn Dodgers officials consulted Dobens and other members of the newspaper's management even before the reformation of the New England League was announced, making sure support for the team would be there. The team's decision to name Dobens president of the Nashua club seemed to serve at least two purposes: the Dodgers assured themselves of having the support of a very influential man, someone who constantly had his finger on the pulse of the city; and, perhaps most importantly, they annexed the best public relations vehicle in town.

After the team was established in the city, but before the signings of Campanella and Newcombe were announced, Bavasi placed a call to Dobens to get a feel for what Nashua's reaction would be if the Dodgers had sent the black ballplayers to the city to begin their professional career. Dobens told Bavasi that all Nashua wanted was a winning team, and that local baseball fans wouldn't care what they looked like as long as they were good ballplayers. It was the answer both Bavasi and Rickey were looking—and hoping—for.

Dobens' role with the team was purely superficial. He had nothing to do with personnel decisions and knew little about the intricacies of running a baseball franchise. But his connections and influence were an invaluable part of the equation, which would prove to make the Dodgers a success both on and off the field.

◆ ◆ ◆ ◆

Newcombe and his teammates recall few problems during their stay in Nashua. When Newcombe and Campanella first arrived in Nashua, the players and their wives were housed in a cozy cottage which was part of the Howard Johnson complex in South Nashua. It was here, Newcombe admits, that he gained a nearly insatiable craving for fried clams.

In fact, Newcombe said the biggest challenge in the city was getting a haircut. "There was this barber, God bless him, who Roy and I went to," Newcombe said. "He couldn't cut black people's hair. Of course, he'd never had to. We'd come back with our hair looking awful. Finally we just said to him, 'Cut it all off.'"

Dealing with opposing players and managers, was a different story.

Manchester catcher Sal Yvars, who went on to play in the 1951 World Series with the New York Giants, reportedly scooped up a handful of dirt and threw it in Campanella's face as he crouched behind home plate during a game in the first month of the season. Whether the actions were racially motivated is unclear. Yvars claims that he was upset with being thrown at by Nashua pitcher George Brown and had thrown the dirt at Campanella's shin guards to express his displeasure. Whatever the case, Campanella sprang to his feet, threw off his mask and charged Yvars.

"Try that again and I'll beat you to a pulp," Campanella snarled.

It was one of the only times that Campanella or Newcombe ever displayed their emotions after being challenged.

"I have to thank God for Buzzie Bavasi and Walter Alston," Newcombe said. "I've wondered many times what would have happened if they said no when Mr. Rickey asked them if they'd take Roy and I up there. There's a good chance that no one would have ever heard of Roy Campanella and Don Newcombe.

"Mr. Bavasi took care of everything for us. We couldn't say anything, but we knew that Buzzie Bavasi and Walter Alston would make sure things didn't get out of hand.

"I remember one game against the Lynn Red Sox. Their manager, (Thomas) 'Pip' Kennedy, was all over us, yelling all kinds of (racial) things at us, and Mr. Bavasi got him into the office and said, 'They can't fight you, but I can. If you have any guts, you'll say to me what you said to them.' Of course, he didn't say a word."

At one point, Bavasi had to be restrained by his own players when Kennedy allegedly said to him: "If it wasn't for them niggers, you wouldn't have beat us."

Newcombe and Campanella could only bite their tongues. They did their talking with bats and arms. And it was no coincidence they were the best players on the team.

"While Jackie Robinson obviously represented the great test case for the Negro baseball player, Roy Campanella, to my way of thinking, did at least as much for the players of his race because of his attitude," Alston wrote in his book, *Alston and the Dodgers*. "Campanella refused to consider himself any kind of symbol; he was just a ballplayer who was glad to be alive with the opportunity of sharing in the good things in life.

"In general attitude away from the game, Roy was a happy-go-lucky fellow. On the field, he was a fierce competitor. ... He loved the game, loved his fellow players, even loved the umpire and the opposition. I doubt if he ever had an enemy in the world."

◆ ◆ ◆ ◆

Before the start of the 1946 season, even before the rest of the team had arrived from spring training, Campanella was taking batting practice at cavernous Holman Stadium and noted the dimensions of the field.

"The ballpark is very large," he said. "I'm not going to try for home runs here. The park's much too big."

The first season of professional baseball at Holman Stadium would be played without a fence around the outfield, meaning any potential home runs had a very good chance of rolling into the row of recently planted pine trees around the perimeter. From home plate, the trees ranged in distances of around 450 down the foul lines to nearly 575 feet in deep center field.

A temporary snow fence would be erected in subsequent seasons. But, as many discovered, Campanella could still hit it far enough within the confines of the park to allow himself sufficient time to circle the bases and beat the throw home.

His much-anticipated debut was not a disappointment—even if the Dodgers lost the season opener, 7–4, to the Red Sox at Lynn's Fraser Field. Campanella went 3-for-4 with an infield hit in his second at bat, a single to right-center in his third trip to the plate and a 430-foot, two-run home run to left in his final at bat. A few days later, in a daytime game before just 600 fans at Holman, Campanella turned in another 3-

for-4 performance in a 4–3 victory over the Lawrence Millionaires.

But as a team, the Dodgers struggled out of the gate, going 3–5 despite outhitting their opponents in all but one game. The downfall was the team's seeming inability to make the proper defensive play: the Dodgers committed 15 errors in those first eight games.

Alston was hardly understanding. He promised that if the current players couldn't get the job done, there would be some on the way who would get the chance.

"Those guys think they've got their jobs all sewed up for the year," Alston bellowed. "They don't know how wrong they are. I want a hustling ball club out there working for me and anybody that doesn't hustle is going to be hustled right out of here."

The Dodgers responded, winning four straight before Lynn pitcher Walker Cress ended Nashua's modest winning streak by throwing a no-hitter—joining Manchester's Neil Saulia as the second NEL pitcher to throw a no-hitter that week.

Even before he had played a game in the New England League, Campanella was being touted as the league's best catcher. And while many of the Dodgers hitters would encounter the season's usual peaks and valleys, their No. 1 catcher was remarkably consistent. He was a terrific hitter, and deadly in the clutch, as the Pawtucket Slaters and Lynn Red Sox would discover in the postseason.

"Roy had no reason to be where he was," said Newcombe, who went on to become the Los Angeles Dodgers' director of community relations and head of the team's drug and alcohol program. "He was by far the best player in the league, without question. But he had to start somewhere."

Though jealousy and racism was not an obvious threat to Campanella and Newcombe, it was never far below the surface.

"I remember one night in Lynn and Walker Cress was pitching," said Bill Sommers, who played second base for Lynn in 1946 before appearing in 56 games with the St. Louis Browns in 1950, his only year in the majors. "Walker Cress was from the Deep South—Baton Rouge—so he had his feelings. But Campanella comes up and hits a long home run off him and you could just see him, he was real mad. I know he wasn't happy about that."

Newcombe became as proficient with his bat as he did with his powerful right arm during his first season in the New England League. Newcombe was called upon in many late-game pinch-hit situations, and more often than not, he came through.

One hit he remembers particularly well helped make Campanella the first black manager to win a game in organized baseball. It was mid-June and Alston had been tossed out of a game against Lawrence by umpire Bernie Friberg at O'-Sullivan Park. The usually even-tempered Alston had told Campanella if he were ever ejected from a game, he'd want his catcher to call the shots.

So with Alston sitting on the roof of the team bus in the parking lot, Campanella called on Newcombe in the top of the seventh inning. Newcombe, making his third pinch-hitting appearance of the week, took a couple of pitches before smashing the ball deep over the center field fence—and into the Merrimack River. The two-run homer cut the Millionaires' lead to 4–3, and Bobby Kellogg's three-run homer in the eighth gave the Dodgers an eventual 6–5 victory.

Nearly 30 years before Frank Robinson was named the

manager of the Cleveland Indians, becoming the first African-American manager in major league history, Campanella already had a 1.000 winning percentage.

Although Newcombe wouldn't have enough at-bats to rank among the league leaders, he had the highest average on the team: 23 hits in 74 at-bats for a .311 average in 43 games. Power was not a problem, either: Newcombe smashed two homers, five doubles and three triples. He drew 10 walks and knocked in 14 runs.

When alcohol prematurely ended Newcombe's major league career, he became the first American to play in the Japanese League — as a first baseman and outfielder.

But long before the glory of World Series championships and Most Valuable Player awards with "Dem Bums," the nickname Brooklyn fans affectionately bestowed on the local ball team, Newcombe and Campanella were intent on helping the Nashua Dodgers be the top team in the New England League.

◆ ◆ ◆ ◆

Dick Detzel will always remember Campanella for his gentle nature. Sure, he could hit the ball farther than anyone Detzel had ever seen, but Campanella always had time for the many children who surrounded the team, including Detzel's son, Richard, who was 2 years old during that magical season.

"Campy, he was a great guy," said Detzel, an Erie, Pa., native who turned down a chance to be a player/manager for a club in Valdosta, Ga., in 1947 to become a high school teacher and coach in Pennsylvania. "He'd have my son up on his shoulders, showing him all around. He was just a great guy to be around."

Detzel was one of many unheralded players on a team that went 80–41 during the regular season and finished 1½ games behind the Lynn Red Sox, only to beat them in the finals for the Governor's Cup, the league's championship trophy.

One of a trio of speedy outfielders, Detzel batted .309 with a team-high 27 doubles. He also led the club with 22 stolen bases.

But his defense may have been more remarkable. In 122 games, mostly in left field, Detzel made 191 putouts and committed just two errors. Center fielder Eddie Yaeger made just four errors while making 258 putouts in 118 games while right fielder Harvey Porter, who played in 100 games, had 144 putouts and eight errors.

Yaeger, who was called "Little Dom" by fans because of his many similarities to Red Sox center fielder Dom DiMaggio, batted .263 with six homers, seven triples and 125 doubles. He also drew a team-best 83 walks. Porter hit .244, matching Yaeger's 15 doubles while hitting six homers and five triples.

The pitching staff was talented and workmanlike. Of the six pitchers in the regular rotation, each went at least 142 innings, with future major league pitching coach Lorne Shepard's seven complete games the fewest on the staff. Newcombe had 15 complete games, while staff ace George Brown went 15–5, going the route 12 times. Dick Mlady also had 12 complete games and a 14–6 record, while Shepard had a 12–5 mark. Jim McFadden (11–7) and Mike Nozinski (9–9) each had 11 complete games.

The infield was as low-key as the outfield, but contributed a great deal to the team's success. Stan Lipka's 25 errors at third base were overshadowed by his .274 average and 60 RBIs. And he almost always put the ball in play, striking out just 22 times in 409 at-bats.

Charles "Dean" Wood started 108 games at second base and batted .252, and the only other player to make the majors from that team, shortstop Billy DeMars, batted .237, but drove in 42 runs and had 42 walks in 98 games.

But one player who seemed to capture the excitement of Nashua and its fans was a French-Canadian at home among his own people: A solid-hitting first baseman named Oscar "Gus" Galipeau.

◆ ◆ ◆ ◆

Trotting down to first base after watching four Newcombe pitches buzz perilously close to his head, Sal Yvars began laying into the first baseman after drawing walk.

"What the hell's going on?" Yvars asked rather vociferously. "He's throwing at my head."

First baseman Walter Alston didn't want to hear it.

"Shut up and get on the bag," Alston said.

Yvars, Manchester's backup catcher, was steaming, but Alston was as even-tempered as always. Alston was playing first base simply because he was the only one with experience at the position. At 34, he wasn't harboring thoughts of a return to the major leagues.

Newcombe was 20 days short of his 20th birthday and throwing heat. He wanted the inside half of the plate, and Yvars objected. He apparently didn't receive any sympathy from Alston.

Stories differ on what prompted the angry exchange with Alston, but Yvars was still upset in his next trip to the plate. He lifted a pop-up down the first-base line that Alston began to settle under near the base line. But at nearly the instant the ball landed in Alston's glove, Yvars slammed into him, sending Alston reeling as the ball landed on the infield grass at Holman Stadium.

Upon reaching first base, Yvars turned around to see where the ball—and Alston—had ended up. But Alston wasn't interested in where the ball was. With all the power he had in his legs, Alston was tearing toward first base to get a piece of Yvars.

"In all the years I was around Walter Alston," Bavasi remembered, "I've never seen him so angry."

By Bavasi's account, and that of a handful of players on that Dodger team, it was a one-sided fight. Alston landed several solid blows before the benches emptied and a handful of Nashua police rushed onto the field to restore order.

Both men remained in the game, but despite playing much of the next month at first base, the end of Alston's playing career was near. The collision had displaced two vertebrae in Alston's back, and a back specialist recommended Alston give up playing.

"It may sound cruel, but that was the best thing that could have happened," Bavasi said. "Our shortstop (DeMars) was taking two steps after catching the ball before throwing it to first. Of course, Alston couldn't see that when he was playing because he was heading for the bag. All of that changed."

And although it wouldn't be truly realized for another nine years, it was the most important break in the history of the Brooklyn Dodgers franchise. It was also a fortuitous turn of events for Gus Galipeau.

The Dodgers, who were off to a 5–5 start before the Alston-Yvars collision, would thrive as Alston became more comfortable in the dugout. And his absence from the lineup gave Galipeau, who saw little action in the first 37 games of the season as a backup catcher, the chance he needed.

After the Dodgers had just 17 hits over their previous four games, Galipeau began adding punch to the lineup. He went 2-for-3 with a triple and home run in his first professional game at first base.

Galipeau would go on to hit .300, with nine home runs and 58 runs batted in in 84 games. He would play in Nashua again in 1947, where he would hit .271, drive in 54 runs, and be the best man at Don Newcombe's wedding.

"The two years I spent in Nashua were the most enjoyable years I spent in professional baseball," Galipeau said. "The fans were wonderful. You'd go to the stores on Main Street and bump into people and they knew who you were. You'd wind up talking to them for half an hour.

"They came out to support us and I think we had a pretty good team on the field."

Whether it was Galipeau's appearance in the lineup, the warmer temperatures of the first few days of summer or some combination of a bevy of other factors, the Dodgers started winning. On June 25, Nashua's record stood at 24–18. Six weeks later, the Dodgers were 19 games over .500 at 56–37, and firmly entrenched in second place after winning 32 of 51 games.

Even then, the best was still ahead.

❖ ❖ ❖ ❖

Given the natural rivalry between Nashua and Manchester—not to mention the competition between the Dodgers and Giants organizations in New York—one would think matchups between the two Southern New Hampshire cities would make for exciting New England League games. They did, but there was something special about the Lynn Red Sox.

In addition to the racial tensions that seemed to play a role in many Nashua-Lynn games because of manager "Pip" Kennedy and catcher Matt Batts, the Dodgers' propensity for beating the Red Sox—including many games at Lynn's Fraser Field—helped make Dodgers-Red Sox games the showcase matchup in the NEL.

"That was a pretty good rivalry," said Donald Chartier, a left-handed pitching standout from nearby Milford (N.H.) High School in the early 1940s who joined the Dodgers in midseason after impressing Alston and Campanella in a try-out. "For some reason, we just beat them more than they could beat us."

It didn't start out that way. Lynn took four of the first six games between the teams and jumped out to an early lead in the NEL standings, but Nashua would win nine of the final 11 regular-season games between the teams. One of Lynn's wins in that torrid stretch actually saved it from a complete collapse in the NEL pennant race.

On Labor Day, 1946, the final day of the NEL regular season, Nashua was within 1½ games of Lynn with a double-header against the Red Sox that day. A sweep and the pennant was Nashua's; anything less and Lynn would be the New England League champions.

Lynn pitcher Walker Cress met the challenge in the opener. The 6-foot-6 ace of the Red Sox staff scattered four hits while his teammates banged out 13 to clinch the pennant with a 10–3 victory at Holman Stadium.

"We always got up for those games against Nashua," said Sommers, who, when he finally made it to majors in 1950, would be a teammate of DeMars. "We always knew that games against Nashua were going to be tough. Each of us knew we were pretty good, and we hated to lose to each other."

The Dodgers' late charge at the Red Sox for the pennant and the accompanying support by the fans didn't go unnoticed by *The Nashua Telegraph's* sports editor, Frank Stawasz.

"Two months ago, Nashua's fickle fandom was swearing at the Nashua Dodgers en masse," he wrote. "Now, it's turned into 'How do you think *we* will do against Lynn?'"

But it wasn't Lynn that the Dodgers had to think about first. Nashua drew the Pawtucket Slaters in the first round of the New England League playoffs and George Brown got the ball in the opener. He didn't disappoint, tossing a two-hitter while striking out seven and walking five in a 1–0 victory.

The game's only run came in the Nashua half of the ninth. Outfielder Bob Kellogg, a late-season call-up, led off with a walk, bringing Campanella to the plate. Campanella shortened up on his bat as if he would lay down a sacrifice bunt to move Kellogg into scoring position, but instead pulled the bat back and sliced a liner into left field. Chuck Nafie charged the ball but lost his footing and fell flat on his face as the ball skipped by. Kellogg scored standing up.

In Game 2, Shepard held Pawtucket to five hits and two walks in the Dodgers' 3–1 win over the Slaters. Campanella's RBI double in the first inning scored Stan Lipka, and Nashua would add two more runs in the third when Wood's RBI single scored Kellogg and DeMars' hot-smash single knocked in Campanella.

More than 5,000 fans showed up for Game 3 at Pawtucket's McCoy Stadium, but the result would be the same. Newcombe threw a five-hitter, striking out five, as Nashua wrapped up its sweep of the best-of-five series with a 3–0 win. DeMars figured in each run: his groundout scored Campanella in the second, he knocked in Wood with an RBI single in the seventh and then scored when Newcombe helped his own cause with a ground-rule double.

With Harvey Porter out of the lineup and his wife gravely ill in a Nashua hospital, Bob Kalbaugh, in his first start of the season, made two brilliant catches in right field.

After making quick work of the Slaters—and Lynn doing the same in a three-game sweep of the Manchester Giants—the series everyone felt was inevitable, the matchup that would determine the winner of the Governor's Cup, was about to take place.

The teams split a day-night doubleheader to open the championship series, with the Dodgers taking a 2–0 win in the afternoon opener at Fraser Field, and Lynn taking the nightcap, 3–2, at Holman, with each game played before about 5,000 fans.

Nashua roughed up Lynn's Roger Wright while Mike Nozinski gave up just three hits for Nashua in Game 1. Campanella had two hits, including a triple, and Galipeau singled and scored the game-winning run on the back end of a double steal in the seventh inning. Nozinski scored the insurance run on a sacrifice fly by Stan Lipka.

The second game was a tough one for the Dodgers to lose. Dick Mlady struck out seven batters in the first three innings and gave up just five hits while finishing with 10 K's, but the Red Sox scored the tie-breaking run in the seventh when Bill Boyce cracked a run-it-out homer to left-center.

The Dodgers got back on track with a 4–2, come-from-behind win in Game 3, and there couldn't have been a better hero. Campanella, or "Mr. Murder" as he had come be known for his postseason success, took a handful of pitches from Lynn's Jim Davis before belting a monstrous 475-foot, three-run homer to left-center, sending the Holman crowd of nearly 5,000 into a frenzy. George Brown retired the side in the ninth to sew up the win.

"There's nothing close to him in this league," *Lynn Daily*

Item sports editor Harvey Southward wrote about Campanella the next day.

The Dodgers fans' joy was short-lived, however, as the Red Sox, boosted by Sommers' five RBIs, tied the series with a 10–6 victory in Game 4 the next night. Lynn scored three runs in the bottom of the third for a 6–4 lead and scored a run in the fifth, two in the sixth and another in the seventh to pull away.

It was the last time Lynn would celebrate a victory.

Newcombe scattered 10 hits and Nashua took a 6–3 win in Game 5 before 4,242 at Fraser Field for a 3–2 series lead. The Dodgers scored four runs with two outs in the sixth, with Wood stroking a bases-loaded, two-run single, Galipeau scoring on an overthrown, and Wood coming home on a single by DeMars.

The next day, Nashua scored four runs on Walker Cress in the first inning and cruised to an 8–2 win and the New England League championship before 3,650 at Holman. Campanella, voted the NEL's most valuable player and a unanimous selection to the NEL All-Star team a few weeks earlier, drove in two runs in the deciding game.

Bavasi announced after the series that the Dodgers players had voted to turn their playoff shares over to Harvey Porter and his wife, who had just given birth to the couple's first child and had undergone emergency surgery to correct complications from the birth. Sadly, she would die several days later, casting a pall over the Dodgers' celebration.

❖ ❖ ❖

In one glorious, unforgettable and historic summer, professional baseball had returned to Nashua. The Dodgers, it seemed, played the role of savior. Nashua Mayor Oswald

Maynard called the baseball team "the best thing to happen here in years," and asked for the team to return in 1947. He also sent a telegram to Rickey to thank him for giving Nashua a winning team.

Campanella would finish with 13 home runs—most of them coming away from Holman Stadium—and send 1,300 baby chicks home to his father after receiving them from local poultry farmer Jack Fallgren in a unique home run promotion. He drove in 96 runs, second only to Manchester's Moe Mozzali's 118. He led the Dodgers with a .290 batting average, had 64 walks, only 28 strikeouts and 16 stolen bases.

By the following spring, Campanella and Alston had moved on—Campy catching for the Montreal Royals, the Dodgers' Triple A team, and Alston managing Pueblo, Colo., of the Class A Western League.

Newcombe, despite a remarkable 14–4 record and a 2.21 ERA in 1946, would return to Nashua for the 1947 season before he, too, would be gone—but not before leading the NEL in wins (19) and strikeouts (186). Reunited in Brooklyn in 1949, Campanella and Newcombe would help the Dodgers go on to win the National League pennant that season as well, as in 1952 and '53.

After being the runner-up in seven trips to the World Series, Brooklyn would win its first world championship in 1955—with Alston as manager. Campanella batted .318 with 32 homers and 107 RBIs, winning the last of his three National League MVP awards. Newcombe went 20–5 with a 3.20 ERA, the second of three 20-win seasons for him. He remains the only player in the history of baseball to win the Cy Young (1956), Rookie of the Year (1949) and Most Valuable Player (1956) awards.

Campanella's career came to a premature end in the winter of 1958 when an automobile accident left him paralyzed from the chest down and confined to a wheelchair. He was elected to the Baseball Hall of Fame in 1969 and died in 1993.

"Roy and I talked about Nashua all the time," Newcombe said. "We always felt so comfortable there. From the start, we were treated like human beings, not two black men in town to play baseball. We felt right at home.

"And everything turned out all right."

Just like Campanella said it would.

1947:
Return to Glory

Nashua baseball fans were happy to see their Dodgers return for the 1947 season, but Don Newcombe was not pleased to be one of them.

He had had an outstanding season in 1946, and while Roy Campanella would leap all the way over the Single-A and Double-A levels to begin the 1947 season at Montreal, Brooklyn's top farm club, Newcombe would return to a league he had already proven he could dominate.

"I didn't think Roy and I should have been there in the first place," Newcombe said. "But I knew why we were there. We had to start somewhere.

"But when they told me I was going back to Nashua, I was not happy. I loved the city and the fans, but I felt I had proven enough and had a good enough season to go on to a higher level."

But in Branch Rickey's grand scheme, there was no other way. With Jackie Robinson due to make his major league debut on April 15, and with Campanella right behind him at

37

Montreal, Rickey wanted to make sure his experiment with Robinson would be successful before rushing other talented black ballplayers through the system. Rickey knew Newcombe had the talent to be an outstanding ballplayer, but he also knew there was no sense in rushing things.

Newcombe grudgingly relented, but not without giving serious consideration to walking away from the Dodgers and returning to the Negro Leagues' Newark Eagles.

Meanwhile, Gus Galipeau was winding down one season while gearing for another. Galipeau, a strapping 6-foot-4, was a standout high school player at Mount St. Charles Academy, a renowned hockey factory in Galipeau's hometown of Woonsocket, R.I.

In 1940, Galipeau was drafted by and played for the Cleveland Barons of the American Hockey League and later went on to play for Toledo and Michigan in the Ontario Hockey League; Atlantic City, N.J., and Baltimore in the Eastern League; and the Minneapolis Millers of the International League. He also spent a year in Paris, two seasons in the Cape Breton League and one in the Maritime League, where he also became the first American to become coach of a senior hockey team.

He was a pretty swift skater, as his nickname — "the Rocket from Woonsocket" — attested. He pursued his professional hockey career while many other baseball players were spending the winter months working odd jobs to supplement their income and recuperating from the aches and pains incurred during the baseball season. And as April began, Galipeau was just returning to the United States after spending four months touring Europe with seven other American Hockey League players.

Galipeau, though, would become a valuable part of the Nashua Dodgers. During the 1946 season, Galipeau appeared in just 17 games behind the plate as Campanella handled the bulk (106 games) of the catching duties. In 1947, with a full season of Class B ball under his belt, he figured to see a lot more action.

Campanella, meanwhile, reportedly received a $5,000 offer by baseball magnate George Pasqual to play one season in the Mexican League. The offer would be increased by $10,000 if Campanella accepted a three-year contract. The offer certainly was worth considering; Campanella made merely $185 per month the previous season in Nashua, plus the rugged catcher was familiar with the Mexican League, having spent two seasons with Monterrey during a dispute with Tom Wilson, owner of the Negro National League's Baltimore Elite Giants.

With Rickey steaming over the intrusion, Pasqual increased the offer to $10,000 per season, but Campanella decided to stay with the Dodgers. He soon received word that he would be making the jump to Class AAA Montreal, a step away from Ebbets Field.

Around the same time, Brooklyn announced that Roy Partlow, one of the first five black ballplayers signed with Campanella, Newcombe, Robinson and John Wright, was released after reporting late to spring training and then pitching poorly. Partlow, whom Robinson described as "one of the greatest left-handed pitchers in the game," immediately rejoined the Negro Leagues' Philadelphia Stars, becoming a footnote to baseball integration.

While most of the Dodgers' lower-classification minor leaguers began to gather in Pensacola, Fla., for the start of spring training, those expected to start the season either with Brooklyn or Montreal assembled in Havana, Cuba. Dodgers management decided it was best to pull their operations out of Sanford, Fla., and avoid a repeat of the racial tensions which accompanied Robinson's arrival for spring training in 1946. The move was a costly blow to Sanford's economy, which, like many Southern cities, had come to depend on an infusion of cash not only from the players, but vacationing Northerners hoping to get an early look at their beloved Bums.

Back in New Hampshire, Nashua Dodgers business manager Alden Clarke prepared his Holman Stadium office for the start of the season. Though attendance was strong in 1946, with the club drawing 62,151 in the league's smallest city, the Dodgers made a concerted effort to sell more season tickets, which were being offered for $50. Frank Stawasz, sports editor for *The Nashua Telegraph*, had headed to Pensacola and began supplying the baseball-hungry hometown fans with daily updates as the Dodgers began their workouts.

In early April, John "Fats" Dantonio, who caught 44 games for Brooklyn in 1945, was offered the job of player-manager of Nashua. The 29-year-old Dantonio had spent seven seasons in minor-league outposts such as Caruthersville, Mo., and Taft, Texas, before finally reaching Ebbets Field in September 1944, when he appeared in three games. He caught 45 games in 1945, mostly backing up light-hitting starter Mike Sandlock.

But after considering the offer and changing his mind three times—the latest change of heart coming just days before the Nashua team was to head north—Dantonio turned it down, instead deciding to be the No. 1 catcher with St. Paul in the American Association.

"I don't know whether I can make the grade as a manager," Dantonio explained. "I naturally think I can, but then on the other hand I had a pretty good season last year and I feel I can profit more by remaining at St. Paul. I also have a family to consider."

Dodgers minor league director Fresco Thompson finally

settled on John Carey as the Nashua manager, albeit temporarily. Carey, who managed the Dodgers' farm club in Thomasville, N.C., in 1946, was considered far too strong a talent evaluator in the Brooklyn organization and was expected to be the team's skipper for only the first few weeks of the season.

Baseball had finally arrived. As Nashua fans picked up their morning paper on April 19, they were greeted by a picture of a handful of Dodgers arriving by train at the city's Union Station. Mother Nature slapped them back to reality the next day, however, as 10 inches of snow fell across the area and forced the team to hold its first workout in the high school gymnasium.

Nearly all of the Dodgers players were in town—all except Don Newcombe, who was already scheduled to start the season opener. But one of those players, Frank Turci, didn't stay long. A highly regarded young outfielder from Bridgeport, Conn., the Dodgers were so eager to acquire Turci that they broke one of baseball's free-agent bylaws by signing Turci on the day of his high school graduation, instead of the day after when he was eligible to sign.

Baseball commissioner Happy Chandler declared Turci a free agent, fined the Dodgers $500 and announced that Turci was free to sign with any team—except Brooklyn.

Aside from returning players such as Newcombe, Galipeau, infielders Dean Wood and Stan Lipka, and outfielders Bob Kellogg and Ed Yaeger, the 1947 Nashua Dodgers were a mishmash of new names and faces. Perhaps the most intriguing player was one who had yet to arrive.

Catcher Ramon Rodriguez, a black Cuban, was signed by Brooklyn in late April and was expected to be sent to Nashua to back up Galipeau while Paul O'Neil recovered from a broken thumb. After the season opener against the Portland Pilots at Holman was rained out, word filtered back to Nashua that Rodriguez was in Boston and would join the Dodgers within a day or two. Two days later, the Dodgers discovered that Rodriguez hadn't even departed Cuba yet; he'd be unable to secure a travel visa until a copy of his contract was forwarded to Cuban authorities.

Rodriguez finally arrived in Nashua on May 9, but his stay—and career with the Dodgers—was short-lived and short on luck. His place on the roster can be verified by his smiling face in the bottom right-hand corner of the 1947 team photograph. But Rodriguez developed a sore arm which kept him sidelined for much of his first six weeks with the team, and then he suffered a nasty gash on his leg while hopping a fence leading to the field. He was ultimately released by the club on July 15 after appearing in just five games and going 1-for-4 at the plate.

Rain proved to be the Dodgers' biggest nemesis early on. The first two games of the season were washed out, shifting the season opener to Portland on May 2. With nice weather finally arriving, Nashua rolled to a 9–6 victory over the Pilots as Newcombe overcame a rough start and scattered eight hits. The Dodgers trailed, 4–1, after five innings before scoring three runs in the sixth and four in the eighth to secure the win.

The second game at Portland was rained out and the Dodgers' third attempt to open their home schedule was thwarted when rain forced the postponement of a game with Manchester after just one inning.

Already the Dodgers were starting to feel the pinch at the gate. Even the threat of bad weather resulted in small crowds at Holman and the team's hopes of turning a profit for the season were dashed before the calendar reached June. Seven of the team's first 11 home games were rained out, costing the team about 15,000 paid admissions and incurring a $10,000 deficit. The Dodgers were looking at a $20,000 shortfall for the season if their luck didn't improve.

Finally, a stretch of warmer, drier weather arrived. It coincided nicely with the heating up of the hometown team.

◆ ◆ ◆ ◆

For an emergency fill-in, manager John Carey was doing a remarkable job. The Dodgers got off to a 13–8 start, battling the Lynn Red Sox and Pawtucket Slaters for the early lead in the standings. But when word filtered down that a permanent manager would soon be named, the Dodgers reeled off an impressive string of victories.

The Dodgers had hit their low point on May 16, getting stomped in a doubleheader by Lawrence, losing 13–1 in the opener followed by an 11–8 loss in the nightcap. But the next night, third baseman Walter King slugged a home run in the 11th inning to give the Dodgers a 4–3 win over Lawrence and snap the Millionaires' three-game winning streak against Nashua.

Newcombe topped King's heroics the next night by throwing a one-hitter in a 1–0 victory over Providence before just 900 fans at Holman Stadium. The Dodgers scored the only run of the game on Ed Yaeger's bases-loaded walk in the ninth.

The following night, the Dodgers got an outstanding game from pitcher Pete Giordano, who held the Lynn Red Sox in check while also driving in a pair of runs in a 7–1 victory. The win was also highlighted by a three-hit game by new center fielder Otis Davis, who lived up to his nickname of "Scat" by legging out a triple.

Earlier that day, the Dodgers announced the signing of

first baseman Lou Ruchser, a smooth-swinging left-handed defensive whiz who was sent down from Montreal after being on Brooklyn's spring training roster. Davis and Ruchser would be prime components, as the Dodgers won 10 of 11 games, including four straight over Portland.

After the first win over Portland, though, there was a changing of the guard. Bob Vickery, a 28-year-old native of Philadelphia, took over the managerial chores from Carey, who returned to his job as Brooklyn scout. Vickery had no managerial experience on the professional level but spent 4½ years as the skipper of armed services teams.

Vickery, a right-handed pitcher who also played in the outfield, graduated from Duke in 1940 and fielded offers from the Yankees, Dodgers and Cardinals. But arm troubles forced him to undergo three surgeries before he signed with the Dodgers and was assigned to Grand Rapids of the Class C Michigan State League, where future major league manager Gene Mauch was the second baseman.

In 1941, Vickery went 6–1 with a 2.90 ERA, mostly in relief, at Fort Worth but was offered a contract to return there for the 1942 season—for $150 a month.

"I was pissed off because I thought I had pitched well and should have moved up the ladder," Vickery said. "I told my dad that I had signed up for Selective Service."

With pro ball on the back burner, Vickery soon found himself in Maine going through basic training with the Navy, although he had hoped to transfer to the Air Force and become an airplane mechanic.

His plans changed quickly one December morning.

"I figured I'd be in the Navy for six months," Vickery said. "Then Pearl Harbor got bombed. Four and a half years later . . ."

When Vickery finally was discharged in 1946 and was pitching at Double-A Fort Worth, his arm troubles returned.

Sitting in the stands one night late in the season after having his tonsils removed, Vickery was approached by Rickey, who happened to be in town.

"How'd you like to manage?" Rickey asked.

"I don't think I'm finished pitching," Vickery said.

He was, however, finished concentrating solely on pitching. After letting Rickey's request sink in over the winter and finally saying he would give it a shot, Vickery discovered just days before the season started that he'd be spending the summer of 1947 in Nashua.

After being given time to get things in order as the Dodgers began their second New England League season, Vickery finally reported to Nashua on May 28. He walked into the cramped Holman Stadium clubhouse at around 3 p.m.

"Oh, boy, you're here," Carey said in greeting Vickery.

The new manager was introduced to the players and handed the lineup card.

"I didn't know anyone on the team," Vickery said. "I had seen some of the guys in spring training, but I didn't get very closely attached to them."

The managerial change did not slow the Dodgers down as Nashua swept a doubleheader from the Pilots on Vickery's first day in uniform. Ruchser had a triple and drove in two runs in the 5–4 win in the opener, while Newcombe improved to 5–1 in scattering six hits and striking out 10 batters in a 14–3 shellacking in the nightcap. Newcombe also had two hits and two RBIs while Davis had another three-hit game and drove in three runs.

"We had a very talented team," Vickery said.

◆ ◆ ◆ ◆

Like many teams, the Dodgers tried a collection of players

in the early part of the season, with mixed results. But the timing of Vickery's arrival in Nashua roughly coincided with the arrival of Davis and Ruchser and a team that was starting to hit its stride.

Ruchser's baseball instincts were far sharper than many of the pitchers'—and most of the hitters'—in the New England League. He had spent the 1946 season at Class AA Fort Worth, hitting .244 with four homers and six triples in 150 games. But Ruchser, who flew 48 combat missions over Germany in three years with the Air Force, played 20 pounds underweight while dealing with health and family misfortunes.

The Long Island-bred Ruchser was invited to Dodgers spring training in 1947, accompanying Jackie Robinson, Pee Wee Reese and Carl Furillo to Cuba. But an unfortunate incident that befell Ruchser inadvertently helped make Robinson find a position and made Robinson's transition into the major leagues a bit easier.

Ruchser was fielding a ground ball from Dodgers coach Ray Blades during batting practice when fellow minor leaguer Marvin Rackley hit a line drive that struck Ruchser in the left temple, knocked him out and forced him to miss part of training camp.

The next day, the Dodgers became the first team to install protective screens around the bases and in front of the pitcher's mound. "My big contribution to pro baseball," Ruchser told *Newsday* in 1996.

Well, one of them. It seems Ruchser was considered one of the top first basemen in the organization and, with Eddie Stanky entrenched as Brooklyn's starting second baseman, the Dodgers were having trouble finding a position for Robinson.

"I figured I had as good a shot (at first) as anybody," Ruchser said. "I never gave Robinson a thought."

But when Ruchser went down and none of the other first basemen seized the opportunity, Robinson began taking grounders at first. When the Dodgers broke camp and headed north on April 10, the team shocked the baseball world with a simple two-sentence press release:

> "Brooklyn announces the purchase of the contract of Jack Roosevelt Robinson from Montreal. . . . He will report immediately."

Ruchser's dreams of playing for the hometown team took another blow in 1948 when another pioneer named Roy Campanella made the jump from Montreal to Brooklyn, forcing a 24-year-old catcher named Gil Hodges to find another position. Hodges would go on to play 1,908 games at first base and hit .273 with 370 home runs in 18 major league seasons.

But in Nashua, Ruchser finally felt he was fitting in. In his first game, he doubled. Three nights later, he doubled in the winning run in the 11th inning as the Dodgers beat Pawtucket, 8–7.

His arrival spelled the end for Bobby Kellogg, who hit .288 in 75 games for Nashua in 1946. After jumping between the outfield and first, second and third base that season, the Dodgers organization had hoped to bring Kellogg along at first base. But Ruchser had assumed a large share of the playing time and Kellogg was sent to Three Rivers, Quebec.

Three weeks after Ruchser joined Nashua, the team was still struggling to find permanent living arrangements for him. After verbal queries failed to turn up available accommodations—and the team faced the possibility of losing Ruchser—the Dodgers took the unusual step of placing an advertisement in *The Nashua Telegraph* appealing to fans to rent a room to Ruchser, his wife and child, who would soon be on their way up from New York:

> *Fans who like the work of the big first sacker know that Ruchser is going to be needed in the pennant drive coming along. If you know anyone that wants to lease their apartment until Labor Day, get in touch with Dodger management at once.*

Ruchser even considered quitting baseball if an apartment could not be found. But whomever answered the ad turned out to be a savior, for Ruchser would hit .273 with 17 doubles, eight triples and nine homers while driving in 70 runs in 96 games. And as the advertisement suggested, Ruchser's bat would indeed be a potent weapon down the stretch.

Ruchser ended his baseball career in 1950 and joined the New York City Police Department as a motorcycle officer. Among his duties during several autumns in the early 1950s was escorting the Brooklyn Dodgers team bus to the Bronx to face the Yankees in the World Series.

◆ ◆ ◆ ◆

Otis Davis, the other new arrival, had something no one on the Nashua roster had: major league experience. Well, with an asterisk.

Davis had spent time in the St. Louis Cardinals organization and played with Walter Alston in Rochester in 1944. He went to spring training with the Cardinals in 1946 but was sold to Brooklyn and played most of the season in Montreal and Fort Worth.

But it was on April 22, 1946, that Davis got the chance he admittedly couldn't have even dreamed about.

"I got into baseball because of my speed," said Davis, a native of Charleston, Ark. "I was a good outfielder and I hit OK in the minors, but I wasn't that good to make it to the majors. I wasn't a big strong guy."

But being a quick guy was good enough for Brooklyn.

After joining the Dodgers organization, Davis had spent time in Brooklyn to have the team's medical people look at a banged-up knee. He was in uniform and on the bench at Ebbets Field that day when the Dodgers were playing the Boston Braves.

"We were down a few runs to the Braves and Eddie Stanky got on base in the ninth," Davis remembered. "The next batter drew a walk and Leo Durocher sent me in to run for Stanky. Billy Herman tried to bunt us over but made an out. But Pete Reiser came up and hit a gapper to score two runs to tie the game. Then we won it in the 10th."

One game, one run scored. The remainder of Otis Davis' entry in The Baseball Encyclopedia is a string of zeroes. Davis returned to the minors, where he stayed for the rest of the 1946 season.

In Nashua, Davis immediately took charge in the outfield. By year's end, he would lead the Dodgers with 24 doubles and a .302 average, finishing 13th among New England League hitters who played in 50 games or more.

"We had a real good team up there," Davis said, "and the fans treated us like royalty. We all did our part."

Davis' baseball career didn't extend too far beyond Nashua. He started at Class A Pueblo in 1948 before accepting an offer to manage at Abilene, Texas, in the Class C West Texas-New Mexico League later in the season. Following the 1948 season, Davis retired from baseball at the age of 27.

◆ ◆ ◆ ◆

By early June, the Dodgers found themselves just 2½ games behind first-place Lynn with a 16–9 record. While the hitting had been inconsistent in the season's first month, the pitching was solid. The undisputed ace was Newcombe, who had built a 5–1 record and, despite his continued unhappiness about returning to Nashua, was bearing down and working on the only deficiency he seemed to possess on the mound: control.

But Vickery wasn't about to let Newcombe think he was bigger than the team.

"Management asked me one day about Don moving up," Vickery remembered. "And I said, 'I think he needs a bit more time down here.' Things were coming easy for him and I think he needed to be knocked down a little bit. He had a bit of an attitude."

What may have been viewed as unhappiness off the field, however, was transformed into sheer determination on it. Newcombe allowed just 180 hits in 223 innings, and though his walks (116) were still high, he struck out a league-best 186, finishing with a 19–6 record and completing an incredible 24 of the 27 games he started.

Other promising pitchers started to emerge on the Nashua staff. Pete Giordano won his first three decisions and Frank Smith, the 24-year-old redhead who was tabbed as chaperone when the team made its way north when spring training camp broke, was 3–1.

Bob Milliken was a strapping 21-year-old who had signed as a free agent down in Pensacola during spring training. He grew up on his aunt's farm in Wheeling, W. Va., and was playing semi-pro ball there when he was discovered by Brooklyn scouts.

"I really didn't want to sign," Milliken said. "But they sent me to see Branch Rickey and, well, before I walked out he had my name on a contract."

In his first year of pro ball, Milliken was enjoying his time in Nashua. He was rooming with four or five teammates in a house at the corner of Main and Amherst streets, paying $5 a week and coming and going as he pleased. It was a lot of freedom, but there was a lot of baseball to be played, too.

"There really were no distractions," said Milliken, who made it to the majors with Brooklyn, going 8–4 as a rookie reliever and spot starter in 1953 and helping the Dodgers to the National League pennant. "We were treated really well and everyone took real good care of us."

By June 1, the Dodgers, like the other teams in the New England League, were required to get down to the 18-player roster limit. Pitchers Aaron "Bubbles" Weisenberg, Mike Santoro, George Souza and Frank Smith, as well as outfielders Joe Bodan and Bobby Kellogg—both of whom had also played for Nashua in 1946—were cut. The team's first left-handed pitchers, Jean Bournot and Clayton Van Cott, were sent up to Nashua around the same time.

Smith's roster move actually turned out to be a trade, with Nashua receiving right-hander Jim Romano from Asheville. Two days later, on June 2, Romano threw a two-hitter in his Nashua debut, beating Lawrence, 4–0. The Millionaires' only two hits were a second-inning single by Lawrence "Crash" Davis and a ninth-inning hit by player/manager George Kissell.

By mid-June, Nashua had six players with batting averages of .280 or better, including Eddie Yaeger's NEL-leading .357. He wasn't a bad defensive outfielder, either.

"He ran down my mistakes," Milliken said.

But while the offense was doing so well, the pitching may

have been even better. Newcombe was the team's best pitcher at 9–2, while Giordano had a 5–1 mark and Romano was 3–1. And Milliken's 3–3 record was far from indicative of his contributions.

◆ ◆ ◆ ◆

The consensus among beat writers in the league's eight cities was that the Dodgers had the best team in the circuit, and Nashua moved into first place on June 21 after a double-header sweep of Lynn at Holman Stadium. Bob Ludwick, a left-hander from West Chester, Pa., made his Dodger debut in the opener, but Milliken's roommate, Dan Horne, got the win in relief when Nashua scored a run in the bottom of the ninth to pull out an 8–7 victory. Bernie Reinertsen shut down the Red Sox in the second game, 5–1.

Three nights later, Newcombe got his 10th win of the season in a 13–1 blasting of Pawtucket, a game that kicked off a string of incredible offensive displays. Nashua closed out June by scoring 36 runs in a doubleheader sweep of Portland — its third and fourth wins over the Pilots in five days. In the 23–7 win in the nightcap, Galipeau had two home runs, a triple and a double and drove in seven runs.

It was quite a return for Galipeau, who had left the team for a few days to meet his fiancee in New York City. Galipeau had only recently received word that his future wife, Nanette, a native of France whom Galipeau met while in the service, was granted permission by the government to enter the country.

"I remember she arrived at 3 in the morning and we spent the night at the Times Square Hotel," said Galipeau, who received $1,000 from the Dodgers to help cover the cost of his fiancee's travel by ship. "We got married a few days after that, and Don Newcombe was my best man."

Yet another recent arrival was starting to make his presence felt in the Dodgers lineup. Outfielder Alan Thomaier got his first hit for the Dodgers in his first game on June 11. He also began pounding the ball when the team arrived in Portland. In the opening game of that doubleheader sweep, Thomaier, who had assumed the role of starting right fielder, crushed a home run that reached the railroad tracks well beyond the outfield fence.

The next night, Thomaier hit a three-run homer but it went for naught as Portland rallied for a 10–9 win, the Pilots' 20th of the season—as many as the team had in the entire 1946 season.

A change of opponents, though, didn't slow Thomaier, who homered in his third straight game as the Dodgers blasted Lawrence, 12–2.

But the Dodgers' hot streak came to a sudden end and a three-game losing streak against Manchester sent Nashua cartwheeling to 5½ games behind Lynn. As hot as Nashua had been, the Red Sox were absolutely scorching, winning an incredible 22 of 23 games.

◆ ◆ ◆ ◆

While Nashua and Lynn were jockeying for position atop the NEL standings, things were not going well downriver. While the Lawrence Millionaires were struggling at the gate, team owner and textile mills magnate George Atkins was seeing his finances dwindle. The industry continued to look for cheaper manufacturing opportunities down South, and as a result, Atkins had trouble paying the bills—and his players. He began selling them off, one by one, making a bad team even worse.

According to reports, Lowell was awarded the Lawrence

Millionaires franchise because of Atkins' failure to meet contractual obligations.

"George Atkins had trouble with money, and I ended up in Pawtucket," said Crash Davis, the Millionaires' second baseman who had played in the majors for three seasons in the early 1940s. "A lot of us found ourselves moving on."

Davis' brother and double-play partner, Hut, was one of those who stayed in Lawrence, playing out the string in the last professional baseball season that city would host. Hut Davis remained in the home he shared with Crash and Crash's wife and young daughter, who stayed in Lawrence while Crash headed to Pawtucket. But when the season ended with Lawrence buried in last place, an incredible 46 games behind pennant-winning Lynn, the usual player exodus was delayed.

"We had to wait an extra week," Hut Davis remembered, "just to make sure we got paid."

Lowell businessman Tom Sellars was given until Nov. 15 to decide whether he wanted to exercise an option to buy the team. The stripped-down product that moved to Lowell played so poorly that Sellars knew very quickly that this business venture was one he wanted no part of.

The Orphans, as the Millionaires were called upon their arrival in Lowell, were doomed from the start. Lowell's baseball fathers insisted that Claude Davidson said he would do all he could to help to bolster the sinking franchise, but that aid was slow in coming.

"Davidson said a lot of help was coming our way. When Mr. Davidson?" wrote *Lowell Sun* columnist Frank Sargent. "The season has about three more weeks to run and all the help Lowell has received from the league you could put in a phone booth and still have room for general dancing.

"What actually happened was a sick baby was left on our

doorstep and everybody in charge ran like hell when we answered the bell."

The Orphans/Millionaires went 6–24 in the first 30 games after moving from Lawrence and word leaked out that Lowell would play its final home game on August 16—opting to play the remainder of its NEL schedule on the road. Team business manager Bob Magill denied the report, but only half-heartedly.

Sure enough, two days after suffering back-to-back whippings (18–2, 15–2) at the hands of the Dodgers, a grand total of 85 fans showed up to see the Orphans get swept in a doubleheader by the Fall River Indians. The attendance was especially embarrassing considering the team had run ads in the local papers begging fans to come to the games.

After Davidson refused to allow Sellars to sign four players he had traveled to New Jersey to scout, Sellars replied by threatening to revive the semi-professional Lowell Stars and take Alumni Field away from the league.

At last, the doomed Lawrence/Lowell franchise had succeeded at something—killing professional baseball in two cities in one season.

◆ ◆ ◆ ◆

The same textile industry worries that forced Lawrence owner George Atkins to foresee the end of his franchise were a problem in many of the New England League cities, including Nashua. Rumors of factory closings forced many baseball patrons to cut back on their trips to the ballpark, and although Nashua was second in the league in attendance, the Dodgers were drawing a mere 1,366 per game, a disturbingly low number in a stadium that could easily accommodate 4,000 fans.

The Pawtucket Slaters, playing in equally roomy McCoy Stadium, led the league with an average of 1,442.

But while the Dodgers continued to struggle to get fans through the turnstiles, the baseball was as good as ever.

Ruchser continued his solid play and began picking up a little extra cash along the way. After going 5-for-5 with a double, home run, two RBIs and four runs scored in a 13–3 win over Lowell, Ruchser collected a $10 bet from fan John Boutelle, who made the mistake of telling Ruchser he didn't think he could hit a homer.

A few weeks later, Ruchser was the recipient of a $50 pass-the-hat collection at Holman after hitting a two-run homer in the sixth off Fall River lefty Bill Eckhardt in a 3–2 Nashua win.

Ruchser struck again two nights later, clouting a solo home run in the opening game of doubleheader sweep of Providence. Thomaier drove in two runs and Davis had a two-run homer in the nightcap, and just like that the Dodgers found themselves right back within striking distance of the front-running Red Sox.

Nashua pulled to within 3½ games after a 10–5 victory over Lynn on Aug. 20. Newcombe won his 18th game and drove in four runs on a double and single. The Dodgers' six-run third inning sent Lynn starter Harry Pilarski to the showers early, handing him his fourth loss of the season at Holman Stadium.

But the Dodgers suffered a serious setback in the game when Ruchser's balky knee flared up and forced him out. The team feared he would be lost for the season after an examination revealed cartilage damage, with surgery the only option.

The Dodgers' bad luck went beyond the field. Stan Lipka, the diminutive infielder who played an important role with the 1946 Dodgers and had played all over the infield in 1947, had to rush home to Canada after receiving word that his infant son had died. It was the second tragedy to hit the team in as many years; the wife of Harvey Porter, an outfielder on the 1946 squad, died after a difficult childbirth at a Nashua hospital the previous fall.

While the Dodgers struggled to keep a steady course, their competition was playing its best ball of the season. Pawtucket, riding the shoulders of a torrid offense and a hotshot pitcher named Norm Roy, fresh out of Waltham (Mass.) High School, matched Lynn's New England League record of 17 straight victories. The Red Sox continued their steady play and maintained their hold on first place in the NEL.

◆ ◆ ◆ ◆

Nashua baseball fans probably never realized how close they came to losing their best pitcher. With the Brooklyn Dodgers struggling to hold on to first place in the National League and woefully short on pitchers, Rickey decided to dip into his farm system to find a fresh arm.

On August 20, scout Harold Roettiger took in the Dodgers' 10–5 win over Lynn. He reportedly was in town to watch Newcombe, who apparently was the man hand-picked by Rickey to make the emergency start in Ebbets Field. Newcombe did earn his 18th win, but it was far from his best game of the season. The right-hander struck out eight, but he surrendered 10 hits and walked seven.

Rickey and minor league director Fresco Thompson were scheduled to join Roettiger and Buzzie Bavasi for the game, but bad weather forced the postponement of their flight up from New York.

Regardless, Roettiger's report must not have been very favorable. Rickey changed courses and dipped into the Negro

Leagues to find his emergency starter, signing a hard-throwing right-hander from the Memphis Red Sox named Dan Bankhead.

Bankhead, one of four brothers who played in the Negro Leagues, began his professional career as a shortstop with the Birmingham Black Barons in 1940, but became a pitcher the next season and went 6–1. He would spend the next four years in the Marines before returning to the Negro Leagues, this time with Memphis.

Bankhead's overpowering fastball was well-known in the Negro Leagues, and in his first year back in the league, Bankhead was named to the All-Star team for the second time. He would be the winning pitcher in both All-Star games that year.

His dominance did not go unnoticed. Rickey heard of Bankhead's exploits and was in attendance when Bankhead struck out 11 former teammates in the Red Sox' win over Birmingham. Shortly thereafter, Rickey struck a deal to purchase Bankhead from Memphis for $15,000, the highest price paid for a black player's contract in 1947.

Rickey knew he was taking a big chance, but his hand was forced because of Brooklyn's pitching shortage.

"I can't help myself. We need pitchers and we need them badly," Rickey said. "I know this boy has the physical equipment to help this club. . . . The only question is whether he will be able to understand the tremendous pressure under which he will work."

Bankhead's major league debut was hardly noteworthy. He lasted just three innings and surrendered eight runs on 10 hits in a 16–3 loss to Pittsburgh. But he did succeed in doing something no other National League pitcher had ever done—he hit a home run in his first at bat. He always was a good hitter.

"I was scared as hell," Bankhead said. "When I stepped on the mound, I was perspiring all over and tight as a drum. I wound up to throw to the first batter and I thought I'd never get unwound."

◆ ◆ ◆ ◆

With Bankhead struggling in Brooklyn, Newcombe and his Nashua teammates were continuing to make a last-ditch effort to catch front-running Lynn. A crowd of 3,077 showed up at Holman—the largest of the season—for a showdown with the Red Sox on August 26.

Eighteen-year-old rookie left-hander Chuck Stobbs had the Dodgers off-balance in the first game, a 3–0 Lynn victory. Stobbs held Nashua to three hits and struck out four while walking two over seven innings.

The Dodgers rebounded to take an exciting 4–3 victory in the nightcap after being no-hit by Lynn right-hander Jim Davis through the first six innings. Thomaier started the rally in the seventh, singling with two outs, and would score on a single by second baseman Jim Massar, tying the game at 1–1. Walt Rogers' RBI single in the eighth gave Nashua a 2–1 lead, but Lynn's Jake Donaldson stroked a two-run double in the top of the ninth for a 3–2 Lynn lead.

Thomaier again got things started in the bottom of the ninth, rapping a triple to lead off the inning. Otis Davis reached on an infield single and stole second before both Davis and Thomaier scored on a two-run, game-winning single by Lipka.

The Dodgers were still within striking distance, but a split of a doubleheader with Manchester on August 28 was costly. In fact, it was Newcombe, who four days earlier had notched his 19th win of the season, who got his sixth loss when the

Giants, bolstered by a two-run triple in the eighth by winning pitcher Lou Lombardo, blanked Nashua, 6–0.

The next night, the Giants' George Bamberger threw a three-hitter in a 2–0 win over Nashua, all but ending the Dodgers' hopes of catching the Red Sox. That same night, Pawtucket clinched third place and a spot in the playoffs with a doubleheader sweep of Lynn.

The faint hopes Nashua fans held for their team to somehow win the NEL pennant were quashed when the Dodgers dropped three out of four on the final weekend of the regular season. The highlight, though, was the awarding of the team's most valuable pitcher and most valuable player awards. Newcombe, with a 19–6 record and 2.91 ERA, was chosen the team's best pitcher while Lipka and Dean Wood were selected as co-MVPs.

Wood, in his second year in Nashua, led the Dodgers with 78 RBIs despite batting just .230. Lipka, also in his second year in Nashua, started the season at second base, moved to shortstop to make room for Rogers and then took over at first base when Ruchser was sidelined with his knee problems. Despite his nomadic existence in the infield, Lipka batted .291 with 17 doubles, six triples and three homers. He also drove in 53 runs.

Each of the three players received a wrist watch presented by Scott Jewelers, and everyone on the team received an unexpected bonus when it was revealed that a Player Appreciation Fund set up by fans yielded each player $70—not a bad score considering it was about half of what the average player made in a month.

◆ ◆ ◆ ◆

With the playoff pairings set and Lynn celebrating its second straight New England League pennant, second-place Nashua concentrated on its opening-round playoff series with third-place Pawtucket.

Nashua knew it would have its hands full in the series opener against left-hander George Kadis, acquired by Pawtucket a few weeks into the season in Lawrence owner George Atkins' fire sale. Pawtucket also received second baseman Crash Davis and shortstop Al Rotermund from the Millionaires. Factor in teen-age pitcher Norm Roy and the Slaters had perhaps the league's most dangerous team.

Kadis had enjoyed a season comparable to Newcombe's, posting a 17–5 record and 2.84 ERA. A control pitcher, he struck out 130 while walking just 55. Opponents hit just .233 against him.

Nashua would answer with Newcombe, but the right-hander simply didn't have it. The Slaters banged Newcombe around for 10 hits (he did have nine strikeouts and just one walk) while Kadis threw a three-hitter as Pawtucket took Game 1, 5–2, at Holman Stadium on September 2.

The Dodgers actually took a 2–1 lead in the seventh when Thomaier reached on a run-scoring infield single and Ruchser, back to full-time duty after two weeks on the sidelines, scored from second on an errant throw to get Thomaier.

But Pawtucket scored four runs in the eighth, the key hit being a bases-loaded triple by first baseman Gene Zubrinski.

In the bottom of the ninth, Kadis threw his glove in the air and walked off the mound in disgust when his first two pitches to Ruchser were called balls by home plate umpire Dave Clarety. Kadis settled down and got the strikeout before getting the final two batters for the win.

Nashua tied the series at 1–1 with an 11–8 win in Game 2, the wildest of the series. The Dodgers scored four runs in the first inning, but Pawtucket jumped on Nashua starter Pete Giordano for six runs in the second to take a 6–4 lead.

Nashua added four more runs in the fourth on two hits, two walks and two Slater errors, before Pawtucket tied the game with two runs in the sixth.

The Dodgers finally put the game away in the bottom of the seventh, scoring two runs on Paul O'Neil's bases-loaded infield single and another when the throw to catch O'Neil stealing second sailed into center field, scoring Otis Davis.

Ruchser drove in four runs in the win.

Nashua took control of the series in Game 3, an 8–2 victory before 7,500 fans at McCoy Stadium. Jim Romano struck out the first four batters he faced and the Dodgers knocked Norm Roy—the Boston Braves' $25,000 bonus baby—out in the fourth inning after touching him up for nine hits and five runs.

Ruchser again led the offense with a pair of home runs and three RBIs. Wood also homered and the light-hitting Massar had three hits.

The Dodgers wrapped up the series the next night, winning their third straight game with another 8–2 decision as Nashua got 16 hits off three Pawtucket pitchers.

The hero? Who else? Ruchser hit his third homer of the series—a two-run shot in the sixth to give Nashua a 6–0 lead—and drove in two more runs while Wood, Davis, Galipeau and winning pitcher Giordano had one RBI each.

But while Nashua was eliminating everyone's pick as the playoff dark horse, the Manchester Giants were pulling off a stunner against heavily favored Lynn.

The Red Sox had little trouble in taking a 2–0 series lead over Manchester. Chuck Stobbs threw a four-hitter in Lynn's 5–2 series-opening win, and Jim Shirley's three-run homer was all the scoring in the Sox' 3–0 win in Game 2.

But a strange thing happened when the series shifted to Manchester's Athletic Park. Catcher John Pramesa drove in five runs as Manchester beat Lynn, 6–3, in Game 3. The Giants then handed Lynn an 8–2 defeat in Game 4 to even the series and send it back to Fraser Field.

Everything seemed to be in place for the Red Sox. They were at home and Stobbs, the West Virginia wunderkind who had a stunning 9–2 record and 1.72 ERA in his first professional season, was getting the ball. But the Giants solved Stobbs and pulled out a 3–1 victory before 2,489 stunned fans, eliminating the pennant winners.

◆ ◆ ◆ ◆

The excitement of an all-New Hampshire New England League championship series began building almost from the moment Nashua fans heard of the Giants' clinching win over the Red Sox. With Lynn out of the way, Dodgers fans couldn't be faulted if they entertained visions of a second straight NEL crown.

But a harsh fact greeted the Nashua faithful when they opened *The Nashua Telegraph* to find a preview of the series: Of the six losses suffered by Game 1 starter Newcombe, three had come against Manchester.

Nonetheless, Newcombe had just enough to allow his teammates to pull off a 3–2 win in the opener thanks to some last-inning heroics. Otis Davis, who had hauled in a deep drive with the bases loaded for the final out in the top of the ninth, singled in the bottom of the inning to score Dean Wood with the game-winner.

Newcombe didn't have his best stuff—he gave up eight hits and two walks while striking out just two batters—but he did help himself with a double and scored Nashua's second run in the fifth for a 2–0 lead. Manchester tied it with two runs, including a home run by first baseman John Lewandowski in the seventh.

As uplifting a win as the Dodgers received in their final at-bat in Game 1, there couldn't have been a more gut-wrenching way to lose Game 2 as Manchester evened the series with a 3–2 victory. Nashua took a 2–1 lead into the ninth, but the Giants took advantage of two Dodger errors to tie the game at 2–2 after a triple by Mo Tortoriello. Tortoriello then provided the game-winning run in the 11th with a sacrifice fly to score Bill Nichols.

The Dodgers got back on track in Game 3 as 4,400 showed up at Holman to see Nashua take a 5–2 victory. Bernie Reinertsen got the win, scattering nine hits and giving up just one run, while the offensive star was none other than Ruchser, who clouted a two-run homer and drove in three runs. Walt Rogers had the other two RBI.

Nashua moved to the brink of its second straight title with a 6–0 victory over the Giants at Athletic Park. Pete Giordano threw a four-hitter and had three hits of his own. But Gus Galipeau provided the biggest blow with a three-run homer on the first pitch reliever Lou Lombardi threw in the Dodgers' four-run sixth.

The anticipated celebration would have to wait, however, as Game 5 was rained out for three straight days. But when the teams finally were able to resume the series on September 16, the Giants received a spectacular pitching performance by Sal Frederico. Frederico, who had the NEL's lowest earned run average (2.37) in the regular season, struck out 15 and walked four while tossing a two-hitter in a 1–0 victory before 4,842 at Holman.

Losing pitcher Newcombe, who a month later would be sold to the Montreal Royals, didn't pitch badly either, scattering six hits and a walk while striking out nine. But Manchester outfielder Joe Bracchitta took advantage of one of Newcombe's few mistakes, delivering an RBI single in the top of the eighth for the game's only run, and sending the series back to Manchester.

For Game 6, it was Otis Davis' time to shine. Davis' RBI single in the top of the ninth scored Lou Ruchser to give Nashua a 3–1 lead, and then Davis sprinted in to snag a sinking line drive with two runners on and one run already in as the Dodgers clinched their second straight NEL title with a 3–2 victory.

Rogers' RBI single in the third had given Nashua an early lead, and Thomaier's home run in the seventh to right-center handed Nashua a 2–1 lead before Davis took matters into his own hands.

After the game, bus driver Leo McGlinchey pulled up in front of the Kernwood Hotel, where the team celebrated with a victory banquet.

As it turns out, the Dodgers may have gotten an extra motivational edge from Mario Vagge. The booster club president apparently promised $5 to every Dodger who reached first base and found himself out of $90 by the end of the night. It was money well-spent, however.

A few days later, the team expressed its thanks to its fans and supporters with an advertisement in *The Nashua Telegraph*:

> *We wish to express our sincere appreciation for the swell way that you fans have treated us during the baseball season.*
> *Thanking you for your generosity and gifts,*
>
> *The Nashua Dodgers Baseball Club*

UNIFORM PLAYER'S CONTRACT

National League of Professional Baseball Clubs

Parties

Between .....BROOKLYN NATIONAL LEAGUE BASEBALL CLUB, INC.

herein called the Club, and ....LOUIS H. RUCHSER

of 7022 65th St., Glendale, L.I., N.Y.., herein called the Player.

Recital

The Club is a member of the National League of Professional Baseball Clubs, a voluntary association of eight member clubs which has subscribed to the Major League Rules with the American League of Professional Baseball Clubs and its constituent clubs and to the Major-Minor League Rules with that League and the National Association of Baseball Leagues. The purpose of those rules is to insure the public wholesome and high-class professional baseball by defining the relations between Club and Player, between club and club, between league and league, and by vesting in a designated Commissioner broad powers of control and discipline, and of decision in case of disputes.

Agreement

In consideration of the facts above recited and of the promises of each to the other, the parties agree as follows:

Employment

1. The Club hereby employs the Player to render, and the Player agrees to render, skilled services as a baseball player during the year...... 194__, including the Club's training season, the Club's exhibition games, the Club's playing season, and the World Series (or any other official series in which the Club may participate and in any receipts of which the player may be entitled to share).

Payment

2. For performance of the Player's services and promises hereunder the Club will pay the Player the sum of $......600.00 (Six hundred) per month, as follows:

In semi-monthly installments after the commencement of the playing season covered by this...

A standard National League players contract, this one for
1947 Nashua Dodgers first baseman Lou Ruchser.

1948:
Banking on Success

A L CAMPANIS COULDN'T BE faulted for wondering what might have been. In 1943, the second baseman appeared in seven games for the Brooklyn Dodgers, making his major-league debut on Sept. 23, but managed just two hits in 20 at-bats.

Before the 1944 season could begin, Campanis was drafted into the Navy and served for nearly two years before returning to the Montreal Royals to begin the 1946 season. But Campanis could see there wouldn't be a place for him in Brooklyn, and his years in the service may have cost him his final chance. At the start of the 1946 season, Campanis was 29 years old, hardly an age to be just beginning a major league career.

After an outstanding athletic career at New York University, Campanis graduated in 1940 and began playing in the Brooklyn farm system, first at Macon, Ga., before progressing to Reading, Pa. (1941), Knoxville, Tenn. (1942) and Montreal (1943), where he batted .294 in 127 games.

But after serving in the military and returning to Montreal, Campanis faced another obstacle: a promising second baseman named Jackie Robinson. Campanis was well aware of the Dodgers' plan of using Robinson to break the color barrier and he wasn't about to put himself in a position to prevent that from happening. Campanis moved over to shortstop, where he not only helped Robinson adjust to his new life, but was a main cog in the Royals' rush to the International League title and the Little World Series.

Campanis, though, knew that his playing career was nearing an end. He had always been a student of the game and became interested in the managerial aspect of baseball. Sensing it was the best opportunity to begin his new career, Campanis accepted the offer to become the manager of the Nashua Dodgers for the 1948 season.

Campanis was joined in Nashua by William Eberly, who would replace Alden Clarke as the team's business manager. Eberly had already spent four years in the Brooklyn farm system, serving as business manager for two seasons each at Newport News, Va., and Danville, Ill. The 26-year-old Eberly was a graduate of the University of Toledo, where he also lived with his wife and young son.

Eberly's introduction to baseball was an interesting one. After listening to a speech by Rickey in Toledo, Eberly approached the Brooklyn boss and asked for a job. Rickey asked Eberly what position he played, but Eberly replied that he wanted an office position. Soon after, Eberly found himself in the employ of the Brooklyn Dodgers.

One of Eberly's first acts as business manager in Nashua was one he probably had a hearty laugh over.

He was having a difficult time tracking down Stan Lipka, a two-year standout in Nashua who was again scheduled to go to spring training camp with the Class B team. Finally, after a number of attempts to contact Lipka by telephone in his native Toronto, he got through.

"I called Toronto and when the voice at the other end answered yes to my query if this was Mr. Lipka speaking, I started right in talking contract," Eberly told *The Nashua Telegraph's* Frank Stawasz. "I talked for 25 minutes before the Lipka at the Toronto end broke in and informed me I must be talking to the wrong Lipka.

"You must want my son, Stan," the senior Lipka said.

But before Eberly could speak to Stan, the telephone connection started to falter. The man promised to have his son call the next day. Finally, Eberly spoke with the "right" Lipka, and the ballplayer agreed to a 1948 contract over the phone.

"But I can't help but think of how close we came to signing Stan's father," Eberly said.

As visions of a new baseball season began coming into focus in Nashua, signed contracts started arriving at the Dodgers' business office. Pitcher Bob Milliken and shortstop James Massar, both Nashua alums, agreed to terms. Campanis, one of the players under contract with Nashua, was already in Vero Beach, Fla., helping Brooklyn farmhands who were early arrivals at spring camp.

But before he headed south, Campanis was one of 30 Dodgers officials in town promoting the team at a dinner party at the Laton Hotel. The new manager made one simple promise about the team he would lead: "You're going to get a hustling ball club in 1948."

Campanis wouldn't have it any other way.

◆ ◆ ◆ ◆

While the Nashua Dodgers prepared to open their minor

league camp in early April, a couple of former Nashua players were making their mark at a higher level.

Roy Campanella, who seemed destined to be kept on the Brooklyn roster when the team headed north, took over for regular catcher Gil Hodges in the fourth inning of Brooklyn's 4–0 victory over Dallas of the Class AA Texas League on April 5. Campanella doubled in the sixth inning and scored on a single by Pee Wee Reese.

Brooklyn manager Leo Durocher was already sold on the stocky catcher.

"He can throw as good as any man living," Durocher said. "I know he's a good catcher, a great receiver. He looked good. The only question is his hitting."

One of Campanella's teammates on the 1946 Nashua team, shortstop Billy DeMars, was also turning heads. After being plucked from the Dodgers' Mobile, Ala., club by the Philadelphia Athletics in the minor league draft the year before, DeMars played well with the big club and there hadn't been any talk of optioning him back to the minors.

DeMars did make the team out of camp as a utility outfielder and a few weeks later he took advantage of an off-day on the Athletics' trip to Boston by visiting friends in Nashua.

Nashua was also realizing financial windfalls thanks to some former players. Milliken, considered by many to be one of the best pitching prospects in the system, was sold to Class AA Fort Worth for $10,000, the largest sum ever credited to a Dodgers farm team for the sale of a pitcher.

But while baseball news was slowly filtering north to chilly New England, the Dodgers were also busy preparing Holman Stadium for the upcoming season. The city of Nashua spent $50,000 to upgrade the stadium, installing 10 100-foot light poles that doused the playing field with 360,000 watts of lighting, placing it on a par with many Triple-A facilities. The infield was also graded and new sod was laid out.

The blood of Nashua baseball fans really started warming when the April 19 edition of *The Nashua Telegraph* let readers know that the Dodgers would be expected in town by the end of the week, having left Vero Beach by train the day before. After reaching Wilmington, Del., the team would take a bus to Cambridge, Md., where it would stay for a few days before completing the last leg of the trip north by train.

And if Dodgers fans needed any further excitement as the season opener drew nearer, the April 24 edition of *The Nashua Telegraph* greeted readers with this headline:

Crack Negro Star Assigned to Nashua

Because of the abundance of top pitching prospects at Montreal and not enough work for all of them, Royals manager Clay Hopper sent Dan Bankhead to Nashua, subject to a 24-hour recall. Hopper didn't hold back on his prediction for Bankhead, saying the hard-throwing right-hander could win 30 games in Nashua.

Even considering the fact that Bankhead probably could easily overmatch the average New England League batter, the prediction was a bit far-fetched. The 26-year-old Bankhead wasn't about to issue any guarantees, certainly not before even one pitch was thrown.

"I sure would like to win 30 games this year," Bankhead said, "but I won't say that I will."

Still, the 6-foot-2, 175-pound Bankhead had far more experience than many of his teammates or opponents. Despite his inauspicious debut in the major leagues the previous season, the Dodgers were obviously still high on Bankhead. They certainly must have figured he'd get plenty of work in

Nashua, and if he dominated New England League hitters, that couldn't hurt, either.

In its scramble to fill a pitching void created by injuries in Brooklyn in 1947, Dodgers officials realized they had thrown Bankhead into the fire without much of a warning.

Now, with a new season, Bankhead would be able to enjoy a new and more subdued preparation for the major leagues.

As the players began arriving in town, so too did the high expectations.

John J. Murphy, a catcher from South Boston, was already being favorably compared to Campanella, In fact, many in the Brooklyn organization believed his arm was even stronger than Campy's.

Outfielder Ted Bartz, snatched from the Detroit Tigers farm system, also came with lofty expectations attached. Campanis put Bartz's throwing arm on a par with that of Brooklyn outfielder Carl Furillo. If that wasn't enough, Bartz was also being talked up as the team's best hitter.

Third baseman Don Hoak, recently acquired from the Dodgers' farm team in Valdosta, Ga., hit .295 in his first season of organized ball the previous summer, with 143 hits, 68 runs batted in and 71 runs scored in 134 games.

The team went through its first workout at Holman Stadium on April 28, and the new manager was already enjoying his baseball dreams.

"Boy, oh boy, I can just close my eyes and picture the field entirely covered with grass under those big new lights," Campanis said.

◆ ◆ ◆ ◆

Surely a pair of blowout victories over amateur teams wasn't worth getting all worked up about. Or was it?

On April 30, the Dodgers crushed a team representing McCartney's Pub, a Lawrence watering hole, 15–0, at O'Sullivan Park, as Bankhead struck out nine and gave up just two hits in four innings of work. The next night, Nashua pummeled the semi-pro New England Hoboes, 23–4, before 1,432 fans at Holman.

The only dark cloud in the weekend sweep came when Murphy broke a finger on his right hand, an injury that was expected to sideline him 7–10 days and leave Nashua with just one catcher, James Salada. But that worry was dispelled when the parent club sent Jim O'Neil to Nashua from Newport News, Va., as the team prepared for its season opener two days away.

Up the road in Manchester, there were some new faces around that city's New England League franchise. Over the winter, the New York Giants decided to end their affiliation with Manchester, and the New York Yankees quickly jumped at the chance to place a team there.

Tommy Padden, a well-known athlete in New Hampshire and a former major leaguer who starred at Holy Cross and St. Anselm College, was named the manager of the Manchester Yankees. Padden, who began his professional career with the Manchester Blue Sox of the old New England League in 1928, signed with the Yankees and played in their system until 1932, when he was traded to Pittsburgh.

After seven years with the Pirates, Padden moved on to the Giants before spending the next two seasons bouncing between the Washington Senators and Philadelphia Phillies, and Milwaukee and St. Paul of the American Association.

The team he inherited in Manchester was composed of 25 players the Yankees moved from their Sunbury, Pa., franchise. New York liquidated that team after determining that the town, with a population of just 17,000, was too small to support the franchise.

A crowd of 3,854 showed up at Manchester's Athletic Park for the season opener between the Dodgers and the Yankees on May 5, but the Dodgers spoiled the new homecoming with a 9–3 victory. Hoak went 3-for-5 and drove in three runs while first baseman Doc Alexson got four hits in five at-bats.

On the mound, Bankhead was a little wild but got the job done. In the complete-game victory, he surrendered just four hits but walked five while striking out eight.

Before the game, Campanis found an empty half-pint liquor bottle on the bus the team had chartered.

"Maybe it's a lucky bottle," the manager said. "We'll have to wait and see."

With the victory, it was settled. The bottle would be making each and every road trip with the Dodgers.

The bottle, though, proved to have no worth at home games. The next night, the Dodgers were baffled by Tommy Gallagher, an 18-year-old left-hander from Somerville, Mass., who shut down the Dodgers for a 4–1 Manchester victory at Holman. Gallagher gave up just four hits (with five walks) and struck out 11 in eight innings for the Yankees, while third baseman Frank Matoh belted a two-run home run.

In an effort to allow late shoppers and store workers the chance to see games at Holman Stadium, the Dodgers had decided to start their Saturday night home games at 8:45. But their first Saturday night outing, on May 8, was anything but special. The Lynn Red Sox pounded Nashua, 9–4, behind two RBIs from second baseman/manager Eddie Popowski.

It was immediately apparent, however, that the feeling that Bankhead would be a winner in the New England League was dead on. On a frigid April night on Massachusetts' South

Shore, only 647 showed up to see Bankhead blow away Fall River in a 2–0 Dodgers victory. Bankhead scattered five hits and two walks while striking out 11 in going the route.

Some times, though, Bankhead needed a little luck.

Several nights later, Fall River ran into Bankhead again, dropping a 5–1 decision, though it was more the Indians' offensive ineptitude than Bankhead's pitching that was the determining factor. Bankhead struck out 10 but gave up 10 walks and seven hits—and still yielded just one run—as the Dodgers posted their first home win of the season on a night so cold that Campanis ordered hot coffee be delivered to players in the dugout.

Bankhead stretched his scoreless streak to 14 innings in getting a 2–0 victory over Lynn in the first game of a double-header split, but many around the team wondered when the highly touted offense would finally start doing its part.

Most of the Dodgers had been mired in terrible slumps. Perhaps the unluckiest of all was outfielder Phil Cardinale, who struggled badly from the start of the season. He finally smashed a deep home run on the first pitch he faced in a game against Pawtucket only to have the game eventually rained out. The rain also cost Bankhead what would have been his fourth win of the season.

But as the weather started warming as the season chugged into late May, the offense started to perk up—and Ted Bartz and Doc Alexson were there to lead the charge.

◆ ◆ ◆ ◆

"Doc and I were quite the 1-2 punch," said Bartz, born Thaddeus Barczuk. "But we had a lot of confidence in ourselves. We had a very good team."

Bartz was a self-professed student of hitting and he had

one of the best ballplayers to model himself after playing 40 miles down the road.

"When Boston was in town and we had an off-day or Boston was playing a day game, I'd go down to Fenway and just watch Ted Williams hit. He was my idol. I watched everything he did to hit a baseball and tried to do the same things. I tried to copy him."

Bartz was attentive to every detail, right down to the Williams batting stance. Bartz said the only thing that prevented him from being an exact replica was that he was a right-handed batter.

"I just made sure I did everything else the same way," Bartz said.

Little did anyone know that Bartz would have one of the best seasons in New England League history. Bartz played in all 125 games for the Dodgers, and in 500 at-bats, he struck out just 33 times. He led the league in batting average (.334), runs scored (115), hits (167) and doubles (42), was second in total bases (265, just five behind league-leader James Pokel of Portland), and third in runs batted in (103, behind Lynn's Dale Long [119] and Pokel [118]).

Andrew "Doc" Alexson wasn't very far behind. The left-handed hitting Ipswich, Mass., resident also played in every game for Nashua, batting .328 with 28 doubles, 10 triples and five home runs. He too was a tough out (just 37 strikeouts compared to 64 walks) and made pitchers pay for their mistakes, knocking in 83 runs.

Bartz actually beat out Alexson for the batting title with a final flurry over the season-ending Labor Day weekend.

"We had an excellent ballclub up there," said Alexson, who like Bartz, streamlined his name, from Alexander Alexopoulos. As for the nickname "Doc," it had nothing to do with any medical aspirations. He apparently acquired the name after he reminded someone of a comic strip character of the same name.

When it came to communicating with his manager, it was almost unnecessary for Alexson to remember the signs. He remembered getting bewildered looks from opposing play-ers—and providing plenty of laughs for his teammates—when he and Campanis would go over game strategy while speaking Greek. Campanis would yell something to Alexson from the dugout or the third-base coach's box and Alexson would acknowledge it with a reply in his native tongue. It made stealing signs pretty difficult.

"With Ted and I and Wally Rogers and Don Hoak, we had a pretty good offense," Alexson said.

"And Bankhead, some days he'd be unhittable."

Whatever it was that helped spark the offense, it became the team's most powerful weapon. The Dodgers would lead the NEL in batting with a .279 average, eight points higher than second-place Lynn.

On May 23, Bartz clubbed three doubles and drove in two runs and center fielder Bob Lee also had three hits as Nashua beat Providence, 7–4. The day before, Bankhead suffered his first loss of the season, striking out just four and giving up eight hits in a 6–1 loss to Portland.

After beating Providence in Nashua, the Dodgers came from behind to beat the Chiefs in Rhode Island, 6–4, in 12 innings the following night. Bartz broke up a double play to allow one run to score and catcher Johnny Murphy added an RBI single. RBI singles by Hoak and backup catcher Joe Soskovich in the ninth forced extra innings.

The Dodgers' dominance of Providence continued two nights later when Nashua roared back for an 11–4 win after spotting the Chiefs a 4–0 lead. And as if the Dodgers' offense wasn't prolific enough, the Dodgers' latest slugger, outfielder

Pete Kousagan, clubbed an estimated 450-foot two-run homer—and added a double and two singles for good measure.

Kousagan, an imposing 6-foot-3, 200-pounder sent to Nashua after struggling at Class-A Pueblo, was a teammate of Bob Lee's when they played at Greenwood (Miss.) of the Class C Cotton States League in 1947. In 120 games with Greenwood, Kousagan batted .301 with 141 hits, 24 doubles, three triples and 18 homers for a team that went 92–38 and won the league championship.

As May gave way to June, the Dodgers sandwiched a pair of unlikely comeback wins around an absolute giveaway.

Nashua scored five runs in the bottom of the ninth to steal an 8–7 victory over Springfield on the last day of May. Light-hitting backup shortstop Fred Gutherz—who, after playing just 18 games for the Dodgers, was released and later became a Nashua police officer—drove in two runs, as did Hoak, Alexson and Lee. Kousagan hit his second homer in three games and Cardinale drove in the winning run on a single.

The next night, though, Nashua blew a seven-run lead and lost, 12–8, to Portland. The Pilots scored seven runs in the fourth inning to tie the game after Nashua had built an 8–1 lead, then scored single runs in the sixth and seventh and two in the eighth.

The Dodgers bounced back the next night, though, as Campanis scored the winning run, pinch-running for newest acquisition Russ Nelson and coming around on Alexson's two-out single for a 10–9 win in 11 innings.

But as the offense was starting to garner much of the attention, Pete Giordano made sure the pitchers didn't get lost in the fireworks.

◆ ◆ ◆ ◆

After enjoying one of his best professional seasons in Nashua the year before, Giordano was on the verge of giving up on baseball. The right-hander, who began the 1948 season with Greenville (S.C.) of the Class A South Atlantic League after winning 13 games with Nashua in 1947, had given serious consideration to retiring. He had started the season with a 4–1 record for Greenville, but his wife had remained at their New York home and he was feeling homesick.

Giordano had notified Brooklyn officials of his intentions to retire, but team representatives managed to talk him out of it. Giordano was happy to move down a level in the Brooklyn chain if it meant he'd feel more comfortable—and closer to home.

Three weeks after heading home and seemingly ending his baseball career, Giordano arrived in Nashua on June 2, about eight hours before the Dodgers were scheduled to host the Portland Pilots in a doubleheader at Holman that night. Whatever rust Giordano may have had from the long layoff, he seemed to shake it off quickly. Pilots hitters never touched him.

Seven batters drew walks off Giordano—the only Pilots to reach base. Giordano struck out just three, but moved the ball around magnificently, recording the first no-hitter in Nashua Dodgers history, a seven-inning, 1–0 victory. Right fielder Bob Lee saved the no-hitter in the top of the sixth, making an outstanding running catch on a long drive toward the fence.

In the top of the seventh, Giordano dug himself a deep hole by walking Pilots Joe Bodan, Paul Gaulin and Hal Mc-Convery with two outs. But the right-hander settled down and got Jim Pokel—one of the league's most dangerous hitters—to bounce out to Campanis at second to end the game.

"Gee, you know I haven't even touched a baseball since I left Greenville," Giordano said after the game.

It was a game Giordano and the Dodgers were quite fortunate to win, because they weren't having much luck against Portland pitching, either. Phil Cardinale missed the sign for a suicide squeeze and laid off a pitch as Alexson steamed in from third base and was tagged out easily.

But Cardinale made up for his gaffe in the bottom of the sixth when his RBI single scored Bartz with the only run of the game.

The Lynn Red Sox took two of three from the Dodgers, but Nashua rebounded by sweeping doubleheaders from Pawtucket and Fall River. As schools let out in mid-June, the Dodgers were within three games of the front-running Red Sox and Pilots with a whole summer of baseball ahead.

What a summer it would be.

◆ ◆ ◆ ◆

As baseball rivalries go, the Dodgers and Manchester Giants had a pretty good one in the two seasons that New York had its affiliate in the NEL. It wasn't as caustic as the Lynn-Nashua rivalry—in which games always seemed to end with raised tempers and steely glares. But given the proximity of the two cities, there would always be a natural competition.

The Nashua-Manchester rivalry took on added flair, though, when the Yankees decided to establish an affiliation there for the 1948 season. New Hampshire, as with all of the other northern New England states, was Red Sox country. There was hardly an argument in these parts about whether

Ted Williams or Joe DiMaggio was the better player. Sure the Yankees were the defending World Series champions and had won 11 titles overall, but there were plenty of New Englanders who had suffered with the Red Sox—and that would make Boston's next world championship that much sweeter, even if it had been almost 30 years since Babe Ruth made Boston the baseball capital of the world.

Nashua Dodgers fans were still Boston Red Sox fans at heart, and any win over a Yankees team—whether it was in the big leagues or down on the farm—was meaningful. So when the Dodgers blasted the Yankees in three out of four games, the rivalry took on a whole new dimension.

Over the four games, Nashua pitchers gave up just 14 hits and 11 walks while striking out 31. The Dodgers, on the other hand, scored 30 runs on 42 hits, including five doubles, four triples and two home runs.

After losing the first game, 3–2, at Holman—despite a three-hitter by Bankhead—the Dodgers posted successive 7–2, 8–2 and 13–0 wins. In that last game, Karl Morrison, who had recently arrived in Nashua with a reputation for having great stuff and excellent control, won his Dodgers debut by throwing a two-hitter. The fiery Kousagan, fresh off paying a fine for using profane and abusive language toward an umpire, clubbed a two-run homer and a three-run homer in the win.

The biggest mystery surrounding the Dodgers was Bankhead. After starting the season with a 4–0 record, he had lost three of his last five decisions, though hardly pitching badly in any of the losses. The Dodgers suffered from a marked drop in run production and gave Bankhead little to work with.

◆ ◆ ◆ ◆

While Ted Bartz and Doc Alexson would eventually spend an entire season battling for a New England League batting title, Don Hoak quietly went about his business. His numbers weren't particularly gaudy, but he was one of the most dependable bats in the Dodgers' lineup.

By season's end, Hoak would have a .283 average with five homers, two triples and 13 doubles, drive in 78 runs and steal 17 bases. His hard-nosed play on the left side of the infield, though, is where he made his mark. He made 34 errors in 89 games at shortstop, but "The Tiger," as he came to be known, was about as tough a ballplayer as you'd find.

Hoak's first love wasn't baseball, but boxing. His career in the ring, however, was short-lived. He was still a teenager when he turned professional, but Hoak lost seven straight fights, getting knocked out in each one. He soon decided baseball was a far more attractive sporting alternative.

While Hoak was a fan favorite for many Nashua baseball aficionados, he wouldn't truly begin drawing accolades until he finally made it to the majors six years later, in 1954. He appeared in 94 games with Brooklyn in 1955, including 78 at third base (sharing time with Billy Cox and Jackie Robinson), and batted just .240, but he played an important role in helping the Dodgers to the first World Series title in franchise history. Two months after that October celebration, Hoak was traded to the Chicago Cubs with outfielder Walt Moryn and pitcher Russ Meyer for third baseman Randy Jackson and pitcher Don Elston.

His time with the Cubs ranked among his worst baseball memories, a team for which he still holds the major-league record for strikeouts in a game with six (in 17 innings). It was difficult for Hoak to deal with going from a team that had capped a 98–55 season by winning a world championship to

The 1946 Nashua Dodgers, the first modern-era affiliated baseball team in the United States to include African-Americans. While Roy Campanella (far right, kneeling) and Don Newcombe (back row, fourth from right) were playing in Nashua, future teammate Jackie Robinson was in Class AAA Montreal beginning his quest to break baseball's color barrier.

Roy Campanella, left, and Don Newcombe
at Nashua's Holman Stadium.

Local poultry farmer Jack Fallgren is surrounded by, from left, Billy DeMars, Dean Wood, Don Newcombe, Gus Galipeau and Roy Campanella. Fallgren offered Nashua Dodgers players 100 baby chicks for each home run they hit during the 1946 season. Campanella clouted 13 homers and sent 1,300 chicks home to his father, who began his own poultry business.

The former Laton Hotel, now a rooming house, located in Nashua's Railroad Square. Roy Campanella and Don Newcombe spent the 1946 season there.

The Bruce Street house which Walter Alston called home during the 1946 season. The house, located one block down Amherst Street from Holman Stadium, was owned by then-Nashua High School baseball coach Pete Chesnulevich.

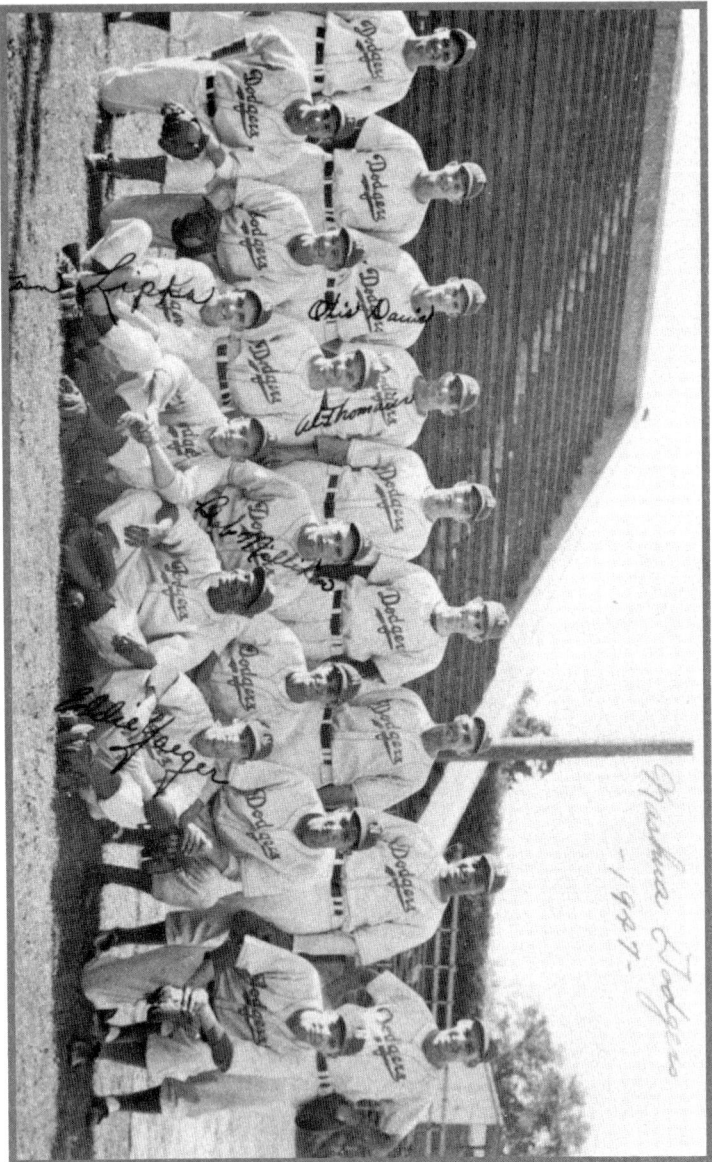

The 1947 Nashua Dodgers included Don Newcombe (back row, second from right) and Ramon Rodriguez (sitting, second from right), a black Cuban who appeared in just five games before being released.

Otis Davis, center fielder for the 1947 Dodgers. He appeared in one game in the major leagues, in 1946 with the Brooklyn Dodgers. Davis entered the game as a pinch-runner for Eddie Stanky and scored on a two-run single by Pete Reiser.

Pete Giordano pitched two seasons with the Dodgers, and threw the first no-hitter in team history, a seven-inning, 1–0 victory over the Portland Pilots in 1948. On the day of his no-hitter, Giordano arrived in town a mere eight hours before the game after being coaxed out of retirement.

Lawrence "Crash" Davis played two seasons in the New England League after appearing in 148 games in the major leagues in the early 1940s. Davis, who was portrayed by Kevin Costner in the cult baseball film Bull Durham, was actually a shortstop, not a catcher as the movie implied. He and his brother, Hut, were a solid double play combination with the 1946 Lawrence Millionaires.

Members of the 1948 Nashua Dodgers, including pitcher Dan Bankhead (back row, second from left). The row of pine trees behind the players are the same trees which now ring Holman Stadium, some of which are now over 100 feet tall.

Dan Bankhead dominated New England League batters during the 1948 season, going 20–6 with a 2.35 ERA and 243 strikeouts in 203 innings pitched.

Al Campanis won a championship in 1948, his first season as a professional manager. He later became an excellent talent evaluator and general manager of the Los Angeles Dodgers.

Ted Bartz enjoyed a remarkable season at the plate in 1948, leading the league in batting average, runs scored, hits and doubles.

Don Hoak had respectable offensive numbers, but it was his hard-nosed style play that earned him the nickname "Tiger." Hoak hit .265 in 11 major league seasons, winning World Series titles with the Brooklyn Dodgers (1955) and Pittsburgh Pirates (1960).

Doc Alexson was one of five Massachusetts natives on the 1948 Dodgers' squad and often befuddled opponents by speaking Greek while discussing game strategy with manager Al Campanis.

From left, Don Hoak, Doc Alexson and Ted Bartz pose in the backyard of the Amherst Street home they lived in during the 1948 season.

The 1949 Dodgers squad included $25,000 "bonus baby" Billy Loes (second row, far right).

Business manager Bill Eberly (second from right) greets manager Greg Mulleavy as he and members of the 1949 Nashua Dodgers arrive in town a few days before the season opener.

Players and fans alike await the start of the first game of the 1949 season at Holman Stadium.

Stephen Eberly, the son of business manager Bill Eberly, poses with manager Greg Mulleavy and players prior to a skills competition at Holman Stadium.

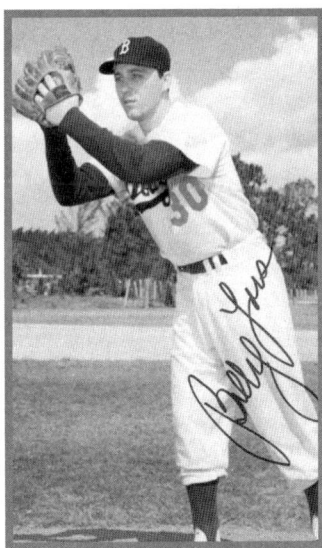

Billy Loes, who threw seven no-hitters during an outstanding high school career in Astoria, N.Y., fired the third – and final – no-hitter in Nashua Dodgers history during the 1949 season. Loes went on to spend 11 seasons in the major leagues.

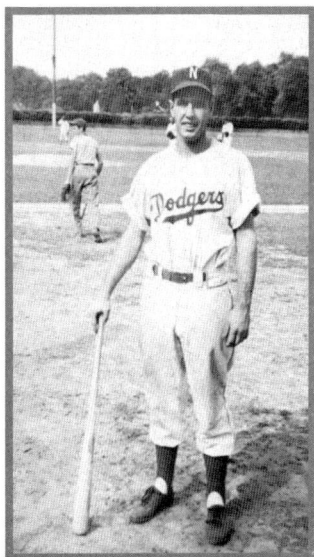

Wayne Belardi was another of the Dodgers' "bonus babies." Fresh out of high school, Brooklyn gave Belardi $15,000 to sign with Class C Santa Barbara. If that wasn't enough pressure, a headline in The Nashua Telegraph *asked if the 18-year-old Belardi could be the next DiMaggio.*

Infielder Bob Kehoe poses with a woman known as Ann, who ran a confectionery shop on Nashua's Main Street where players often hung out.

Dodgers infielder Bob Kehoe was considered one of the best athletes ever to come out of St. Louis. He excelled in baseball, soccer and basketball and was elected to the St. Louis Amateur Baseball Hall of Fame in 1999.

Players pose alongside the team bus outside Holman Stadium before heading off for a road game. Connie Heard, the fourth African-American to don a Nashua Dodgers uniform, can be seen in the back row, third from left.

Future major leaguer Billy Hunter, right, has a little fun at Wayne Belardi's expense outside the Dodgers' Holman Stadium clubhouse.

Dodgers players, from left, Don Taylor, J.J. Murphy, Bob Kehoe, Norm Postolese and Bill Samson enjoy a night on the town at a Boston nightclub.

Bob Brown (left) and Billy Hunter (second from left) find an interesting place to pose for this photo with two unidentified teammates in downtown Providence in 1949.

From left, Don Taylor, Norm Postolese and J.J. Murphy pool their wealth while relaxing at a park at the top of Library Hill in Nashua.

The Dodgers' own Murderers' Row. From left, Rudy Antonetz, Norm Postolese, Wayne Belardi, Billy Hunter (kneeling), J.J. Murphy and Don Taylor. Postolese hit his only home run on the final day of the 1949 season—the last one hit by a Nashua Dodger.

An aerial view of Holman Stadium, some 50 years after the Dodgers left town.

a team that finished nine games under .500 and was 47 years removed from its last championship.

"Don Hoak played for the Brooklyn Dodgers, a very good baseball team, before he was traded to the Cubs, a very bad one," said Jim Brosnan, a writer who also pitched for the Cubs for three-plus seasons. "It was hard for Hoak to relate. As far as he was concerned, he went right from Brooklyn to Pittsburgh (to whom he was traded in November 1956) without ever stopping in Chicago.

"He refused to accept that he was a Cub," Brosnan added. "He had nothing but obscene words for the Cubs and their organization; he even hated (club owner) P.K. Wrigley.

"Hoak is quite possibly the only man who ever conquered his Cubness."

Brosnan was referring to the "hex" cast on former Cubs ballplayers, who seemingly languished among baseball's also-rans after appearing in home whites at Wrigley Field. Few former Cubs were ever able to go on to enjoy baseball success. Hoak was one an exception, moving on to the Pittsburgh Pirates the following season.

Though he played an unfortunate role in Harvey Haddix's unsuccessful bid for a perfect game on May 26, 1959—committing an error on Felix Mantilla's ground ball in the 12th inning, which started the Boston Braves' winning rally—he would play a vital role for the Pirates the next season. Hoak finished second to teammate Dick Groat for National League Most Valuable Player honors after hitting .282 with 16 home runs, 79 RBIs and 97 runs scored, and helped Pittsburgh beat the New York Yankees for the 1960 World Series title.

He had conquered his "Cubness."

While still a Dodgers farmhand, Hoak dabbled in political history in 1951, though he wouldn't know it at the time. Playing in a Winter League game in Havana shrouded by a student uprising, Hoak was at bat when one of the protesting students ran to the pitcher's mound and grabbed the ball. The student threw two pitches to Hoak, who fouled them off, before police rushed onto the field and apprehended the student.

The student? Fidel Castro.

"With a little work on his control, Fidel Castro would have made a better pitcher than prime minister," Hoak once said.

Hoak was involved in two other bizarre plays during his career. While with the Cincinnati Reds in 1957, Hoak was on second base and Gus Bell was on first in a game against the Milwaukee Braves. Wally Post grounded the ball toward shortstop, but Hoak, who was on his way to third, fielded the ball himself and flipped it to stunned Braves shortstop Johnny Logan. Hoak was ruled out for getting hit with a batted ball, the third such incident involving the Reds that season. It prompted NL president Warren Giles and AL counterpart Will Harridge to jointly announce a rule change that declared that both the base runner and batter would be called out on any similar plays, with no other runners allowed to advance.

The "Don Hoak Rule" was born.

Hoak prided himself as a student of the game and spent long hours reading the rule book. His knowledge would come in handy when he was with the Pirates. Hoak was on third base in a game in 1961 when the batter hit a long drive down the line and Hoak ran toward the plate. After the umpire ruled the ball foul, Hoak did not return to third base, instead standing a step away from home plate.

When the umpire asked Hoak what he was doing, Hoak said he was taking his lead. He knew there was no rule that required he return to third base, and there was certainly no rule that limited the lead he could take. So the umpire had no choice but to throw a new ball to the pitcher . . . at which point Hoak took a stride and stepped on the plate for a run, effectively stealing home.

Shortly thereafter, another rule change was passed stating that base runners had to return to their original base after a foul ball.

Even Hoak's death came in bizarre circumstances. After managing Columbus, the Pirates' Triple-A affiliate, to the International League finals in 1969, the fiery Hoak suffered a heart attack and died while chasing his brother-in-law's stolen car on Oct. 9, 1969—the same day the Pirates hired Danny Murtaugh as manager, a position Hoak had hoped to land himself.

◆ ◆ ◆ ◆

The arrival of two new faces in Nashua—shortstop Billy Kearns of Watertown, Mass., and outfielder George Boston, a Swampscott, Mass., native and standout at Boston University—gave the Dodgers five ballplayers who called Massachusetts home, joining Alexson (Ipswich), J.J. Murphy (South Boston) and Joe Soskovich (Holyoke).

Both Kearns and Boston saw their first action for Nashua on June 22, but neither played much of a role in the Dodgers' 5–2 victory over Lynn, a win that pulled Nashua to within a game of the first-place Red Sox. The victory was the fourth of an eventual seven-game streak.

But the win wasn't without its fireworks. Campanis, who was placed on the inactive list before the game to make room on the roster for Kearns, was not happy with the work of umpires Jim Duffy and Hank Soar. Campanis rode Duffy so hard that when Campanis came out to argue a particular call, Duffy wagged his finger in front of Campanis' face before ejecting him.

Campanis was fuming. A few innings later, Soar halted the game when he suspected Campanis was calling plays from the ramp leading to the Dodgers' locker room.

But as the Dodgers enjoyed their winning streak, a bit of bad news surfaced. Bankhead, suffering from a sore arm, was given an extra day's rest. It didn't help, though, as he was the losing pitcher in a 5–3 loss to Springfield in the second game of a doubleheader.

Bankhead's injury was one of a handful of bumps and bruises that plagued Nashua. Karl Morrison, who won his third game of the season and drove in the only run in the Dodgers' 1–0 victory in the opener, was forced to play third base after Bartz had a toenail removed, while Murphy moved out from behind the plate to play left as Kousagan sat out with a bruised rib after being hit by a pitch.

But while Bankhead was struggling, Morrison was proving to be a real find. In his first four starts (all wins) for Nashua, Morrison had three shutouts and had allowed just one earned run in 36 innings pitched. His streak of scoreless innings reached 27 innings and he had 31 strikeouts and gave up just 11 hits.

◆ ◆ ◆ ◆

Despite the obvious love Nashua fans had for the Dodgers, not every decision Campanis made gained the approval of the Holman faithful.

On June 28, in a game against Portland in Nashua, Campanis elected to bring Kousagan in to pinch-hit for Kearns with Nashua trailing, 3–1, with a runner on and two outs in the ninth inning. Portland starter Carl Kolosna was dominating the Dodgers, surrendering just four hits while striking out 14 batters, including each of Nashua's 10 hitters in the lineup at least once.

Campanis figured Kearns, who hit just .163 in 12 games for Nashua before being released, wouldn't have much of a chance against the King, as Kolosna was called. Why not bring in Kousagan, who was leading the team in home runs? He was a free swinger, but with Kolosna certain to be throwing heat, one swing could tie the game.

The strategy didn't exactly pan out. Kousagan watched as strike three crossed the plate, ending the contest and giving Kolosna his 15th strikeout of the game. The fans booed and Kousagan argued the call vehemently and somehow got thrown out of a game that was already over.

A few days later, local attorney John D. Warren penned an interesting verse:

> *When Kosloski batted for Sweeney, Sullivan left*
> *   the park*
> *When 'Casey at the Bat' struck out, Mudville lived*
> *   in the dark;*
> *In the great American game, one always lives and*
> *   learns,*
> *But I never thought I'd live to see Kousagan batting*
> *   for Kearns*

Kousagan had already gained the reputation for being a boisterous, somewhat disruptive force on the Dodgers. He also didn't agree with many of Campanis' decisions—and wasn't afraid to let the manager know.

But despite his proclivity for the long ball—he hit nine homers in 34 games and would finish second only to Bartz's 16 in 125 games—the slugger had clearly worn out his welcome. On July 5, the Dodgers activated outfielder Phil Cardinale and outrighted Kousagan to Three Rivers of the Canadian-American League.

Kousagan wanted no part of playing in the CAL. He packed up his things, trudged down to Nashua's Union Station and purchased a one-way ticket to his hometown of Akron, Ohio.

Kousagan "talked his way out of Nashua, and didn't strike his way out, as some might insist," wrote *The Nashua Telegraph*'s Stawasz in the days following the outfielder's release.

A few days later, one of the fans' better traditions was scrapped when it was decided to halt the practice of passing a hat through the stands when a Dodgers player a hit home run at Holman. There were nights when players would earn a $50 or $60 windfall for a long ball—a pretty good chunk of change when the average contract was paying around $160 a month.

Despite a suffering economy in Nashua (and many other mill towns) that took a bite out of many fans' disposable income, the rationale was quite simple.

"The purses we gave to the players were ill-advised," one fan said. "It encouraged the players to swing from the heels and for the fences instead of trying for base hits that would win ball games."

Fans decided to concentrate their efforts on an end-of-season gift. After the 1947 season, each player was presented with a brand new wallet stuffed with $75 in cash. At the conclusion of the 1948 season, fans hoped to double that amount.

◆ ◆ ◆ ◆

As the summer heat arrived, the Dodgers found themselves with a frighteningly short supply of pitching. In addition to sore arms keeping just about everyone on the staff out of games here and there, Nashua soon found itself dealing with injuries and missing hurlers.

Giordano was considered AWOL when he failed to return to Nashua after a trip back home to New York. The club had granted Giordano permission to go with the expectation that he return several days later. But nearly four days after he was supposed to be back in Nashua, Giordano couldn't be found.

Eberly had planned to suspend the right-hander for his tardiness before he arrived later in the day. But because of the skeletal pitching staff, Eberly was forced to keep Giordano on hand.

Three days later, though, things got worse for the Dodgers.

In the first inning of the Dodgers' eventual 6–5 loss to Pawtucket on July 10, Tony Sierzega, a right-hander with a 3–0 record, was struck on the pitching hand with a line drive. He knew immediately that the hand was broken but he made his teammates promise not to tell Campanis about it.

Despite the obvious pain—and a pretty good job of hiding the swollen hand from Campanis in the dugout—Sierzega lasted into the ninth inning before he was replaced by Bankhead. Bankhead, though, gave up a game-winning, 360-foot double to Slaters outfielder Bob Montag.

Pitchers weren't the only ones suffering injuries, however. In the same game, Hoak was injured in a collision with Pawtucket's Jake Weisenberger at second base. College football fans would surely recognize Weisenberger, who scored three touchdowns for Michigan in a 49–0 victory over Southern Cal in the 1948 Rose Bowl. Hoak returned to the lineup the next day.

Two nights later Morrison was an emergency starter because another pitcher, Bob Ludwick, didn't make it back from a visit home to West Chester, Pa., in time to start. Morrison, who after a dazzling start had been struggling, suffered his first loss of the season as Pawtucket rolled to a 7–1 win.

With Sierzega's injury expected to keep him sidelined for a while, the Dodgers entered an important three-game series against Portland with just six pitchers. It didn't matter in the opener, in which Nashua won, 6–4, to close within 3½ games of the Pilots and a half-game of the Red Sox. The Dodgers benefited from four errors to score four runs in the eighth inning, but Giordano had to come on in relief of Bill Samson in the bottom of the inning after Portland scored three runs of its own.

Preservation of the beaten-up pitching staff, though, took precedence the next night when Ludwick was shelled for six runs in the first inning. Campanis pulled Cardinale in from center field, and Cardinale responded with eight-plus innings, striking out seven, but walking 11 and throwing two wild pitches. Alexson also saw action on the mound in the Dodgers' 13–6 loss.

Despite the obvious manpower shortage, the Dodgers somehow began pulling things together. After Portland left town, Nashua got an outstanding game from Bankhead, who struck out 16 while allowing just four hits in blanking Manchester, 4–0, at Athletic Field. Bankhead helped himself with a two-run homer.

The next night, after an 8–0 loss in the opener of a doubleheader against Lynn—and losing Morrison to a pulled back muscle in the process—Nashua bounced back with a 10-run first inning en route to a 13–3 win, with Mike Quill going the distance for his eighth win.

The Dodgers' offense did its part the following day, scoring four runs with two outs in the bottom of the ninth inning to pull out an 11–10 win as Lee had a homer and four RBIs.

Bankhead won his 10th game of the season with another

four-hitter, beating Providence, 5–3. In his next start, Bankhead followed that with a three-hitter and got plenty of support in the Dodgers' 12–1 victory over Springfield. He continued to battle wildness (eight walks), but his 10 strike-outs helped keep many of those baserunners from advancing.

If opponents had noticed Bankhead getting stingier with the hits he allowed, Springfield would find him downright untouchable his next time out.

In the first game of a doubleheader against the Cubs, Bankhead threw a seven-inning no-hitter, although a couple of walks and an error prevented him from getting the shutout in a 13–1 win. But if becoming the second Dodgers pitcher of the season to throw a no-hitter wasn't notable enough, Bankhead bailed his team out of a tenuous situation in the nightcap and threw $1\frac{2}{3}$ innings of hitless relief in an 11-in-ning, 4–3 win.

With the two wins, Bankhead had put together seven straight victories and improved his record to 13–5. In $143\frac{2}{3}$ innings, Bankhead had an incredible 160 strikeouts and had allowed just 83 hits, but his 94 walks still were reason for concern.

Despite his sacrifice and risk of injury for the team, Bankhead didn't endear himself to Campanis by pulling out of his next start, forcing the manager to pitch the recently ac-quired Chet Beres in a 6–2 loss to Lynn. His arm was indeed sore, but the Dodgers, still struggling with just six pitchers, didn't have a lot of leeway.

"It wasn't the first time (Bankhead) had excused himself from a pitching assignment, but it will be the last," Stawasz wrote the next day. "Manager Al Campanis told his short-handed pitching staff that hereafter pitching assignments will be taken as handed out, not as suited to the individual hurler."

The Dodgers finally got a much-needed shot in the arm to

close out July when Ludwick threw a six-hitter in a 5–3 victory over Manchester, snapping the Yankees' four-game winning streak and the Dodgers' three-game losing streak. The win came on the heels of a heartbreaking doubleheader sweep to Lynn in which Don Falling threw a one-hitter (his third straight shutout win over Nashua) in the opener and Red Sox first baseman Dale Long clubbed a grand slam in the bottom of the ninth to give Lynn the win.

Even after the Red Sox took all three games against the Dodgers, Mario Vagge decided a beaten team didn't necessarily have to be a hungry one. The fan club president had promised to treat the Dodgers to a chicken dinner should they take two of three in Lynn. They came home without a win, but went home with full bellies when Vagge picked up the tab anyway.

In early August, Nashua's baseball team began enjoying its most torrid streak of the season. And everyone, it seemed, did his part.

First Nashua took three straight from Manchester, with Alexson picking up two boxes of cigars from a Manchester tobacco dealer for a pair of three-run homers; Bankhead striking out 15 batters in getting his 14th win of the season; Hoak going 4-for-4 in a 5–1 win over the Yankees—and the Dodgers family growing by one when J.J. Murphy's wife gave birth to a daughter, Jeanne Patricia Murphy.

Next up were the Pawtucket Slaters, who provided little resistance in dropping a pair of doubleheaders to the Dodgers. Russ Nelson went 3-for-3 with four RBI to win one game, then laid down a perfect suicide squeeze bunt in the bottom of the ninth of the next game to score Bob Lee (who had roped a two-run triple to tie the game) in a 5–4 win.

Even Pawtucket turning a triple play—the third the Dodgers had been involved in that season—wasn't enough to halt the Dodgers' momentum, although a 14–14 tie with the Slaters technically ended the Dodgers' winning streak at seven games. In that tie, Nashua scored nine runs in the sixth inning to erase a 13–4 deficit, using one hit and five walks by Slaters starter Don Liddle.

The Slaters would take a 14–13 lead in the top of the seventh, but Nashua tied it in the bottom of the inning when Bankhead—playing left field after Lee was beaned in the sixth—drew a walk, was sacrificed to second, and scored on an error.

A night later, it was Walt Rogers who stepped into the spotlight. After going 4-for-5 with three RBIs in a 12–1 Nashua win in the first game of a doubleheader against Fall River, the infielder blasted two homers and drove in four runs as Nashua banged out 15 hits in a 17–7 throttling of the Indians in the nightcap. Pitcher Bill Samson, who saw action at third base in the opener, smacked a three-run homer while playing first base in the second game.

The six homers the Dodgers hit in the sweep gave Nashua a team-record 48 for the season, four better than the 1947 team—with a month still to go in the season.

Bankhead turned in his second 15-strikeout game (in his last three starts) in Nashua's 6–2 win over Manchester to stretch the unbeaten streak to 12 games before the Yankees finally slowed Nashua down with a 6–2 win at Holman.

But while different Dodgers took their turns playing the role of hero, one of Nashua's most remarkably consistent players was Alexson. He got his 19th and 20th doubles of the season in the loss to Manchester. The next night, in a doubleheader split with Pawtucket, he stroked two doubles and two triples, and then pitched in the Dodgers' loss in the second game.

"He was a great player," Giordano said. "He could hit like

you wouldn't believe. Just drove the ball. And he had one of the best gloves at first base I had ever seen."

While Alexson was the anchor of an outstanding offensive machine, Bankhead was far and away the best pitcher on the Dodgers' staff. In fact, he was the most dominating pitcher in the NEL.

The right-hander followed up his two 15-strikeout games with a 14-K affair, throwing a three-hitter (one of those, un-fortunately, being a two-run homer) in a 5–3 Nashua win, Bankhead's 17th win of the season. Bankhead struck out seven straight Slaters at one point and the three hits and three runs he allowed all came in the eighth inning.

Bankhead carried the staff through its most difficult stretches earlier in the season when injuries and general in-effectiveness haunted the Dodgers. But as the season entered the final home stretch, others began to pick up the slack.

A prime example of that came the night after Bankhead's win when Chet Beres and Mike Quill each tossed three-hit-ters as Nashua won a pair of 2–1 games in a sweep of Fall River. For Quill, it was his 11th win of the season.

Soskovich—"The platinum-haired half of the catching staff," as Stawasz called him—went 2-for-3 and scored two runs, while his solo home run in the seventh inning provid-ing the difference in the second game.

After an incredible streak in which the Dodgers won 16 of 18 games, Nashua found itself just two games behind second-place Portland and 5½ back of front-running Lynn. With just over three weeks remaining in the season, the Dodgers were right back where they wanted to be.

◆ ◆ ◆ ◆

On August 13, New England League fans knew hits would

be at a premium when the Dodgers' Bankhead was matched up against the Portland Pilots' Carl Kolosna. In addition to this showdown between two of the league's top pitchers, it was a very important game for both teams.

The Pilots were trying to stay within striking distance of Lynn, while at the same time trying to stave off the fast-rising Dodgers. Red-hot Nashua, on the other hand, was beginning to view Portland merely as another hurdle on its way to catching the Red Sox and winning the New England League pennant for the first time.

It wouldn't be easy for the Dodgers. Aside from Bankhead, no NEL pitcher struck out more batters than Kolosna's 201 in 1948. The Pilots' ace was clearly one of the league's best pitchers, compiling a 16–5 record (with 15 complete games) and 2.72 ERA in 29 appearances. He struck out more than twice as many batters as he walked (99) in 182 innings pitched and gave up just 120 hits and 55 earned runs.

Three starts prior to the Nashua-Portland game, Kolosna had thrown a no-hitter against Lynn, winning a 5–0 game in seven innings just six days after Bankhead had thrown his no-hitter against Springfield. Kolosna's was the third no-hitter of the season in the New England League.

The Dodgers knew all too well about the proficiency of "King" Kolosna on the mound. Back in June, Kolosna struck out 15 Nashua batters, including the temperamental Pete Kousagan to end the game. Unfortunately for the Dodgers, Kolosna was showing signs of another outstanding game.

But Bankhead was far from being overshadowed. The Pilots reached the right-hander for a few hits early in the game, but as the innings passed, Bankhead seemed to be getting stronger. With the game still scoreless, Bankhead struck out the side in the sixth inning.

After Kolosna set down the Dodgers in the bottom of the

inning, Bankhead struck out the side again in the seventh. Kolosna, who was working on a no-hitter, would encounter his trouble in the bottom of the seventh.

Hoak reached on a walk—Kolosna's only free pass of the night—and moved to second on a sacrifice by Alexson. He advanced to third on a passed ball before Soskovich, who had replaced Bartz in the outfield after Bartz was ejected in the fifth inning for shoving umpire Bernie Friberg, ripped a double to score Hoak and give the Dodgers a 1–0 lead.

Kolosna got the final out, sending the Pilots back to the plate.

Bankhead—who would end the game with 14 strikeouts, his fourth game with at least that many K's this season—proceeded to strike out the next two hitters before the third batter grounded out to end the string of strikeouts at eight.

An article on the game in *The Nashua Telegraph* the next day made no mention of the eight straight strikeouts, but at the time no pitcher in organized baseball had recorded such a feat. In fact, the major league record for consecutive strikeouts at the present pitching distance was seven, set in 1906 by George Wiltse of the New York Giants, and tied by Brooklyn's Dazzy Vance in 1924 and Van Lingle Mungo, also of the Dodgers, in 1936.

The Dodgers won the showdown, 1–0. It was a heartbreaking loss for Kolosna, who struck out 11.

For Bankhead, it was his 18th win of the season.

The next night, the Dodgers would overtake the Pilots for second place, and Soskovich would be in the middle of it all again. His two-run single capped a four-run rally in the ninth as Nashua pulled out a 7–5 win over Portland, making a winner of the gritty Samson, who had to go into the stands during the fifth inning to have his dislocated finger reset by a doctor. Cardinale had four RBIs in the win, which pulled the

Dodgers within two games of Lynn, which had dropped a 9–7 decision to Manchester.

After the game, and much to the delight of some of his former teammates, word filtered back to Nashua that Don Newcombe had pitched the first no-hitter of his career in Montreal's 8–0 seven-inning victory over Toronto in the second game of an International League doubleheader.

But the news was not all good. A check of numbers showed that attendance at Dodgers games was well below the 1947 average—and that team had a bevy of rainouts to deal with. Dodgers officials, seeing the struggling economy not only in Nashua but in much of the Northeast—including most all of the New England League cities—were worried.

◆ ◆ ◆ ◆

Back on the field, Nashua found more creative ways of winning—and from more unlikely sources.

After Campanis had seen enough of Quill and Ludwick getting shelled in the early going of a game against Providence, he turned to Beres. And while his teammates pushed across seven runs in the bottom of the third inning, Beres yielded just one earned run over 6$^1/_3$ innings as the Dodgers posted a wild 13–9 victory over the Chiefs and moved within a game of the Red Sox.

The Dodgers had 17 hits and took advantage of nine walks. Hoak had another four-hit game while Cardinale and Soskovich had three RBIs each.

Nashua left the Ocean State with more than a victory, too, picking up submarine thrower Charlie Bird, whom the Chiefs released before the game. He had been the ace of the Providence staff, and although he was well into his 30s, the Dodgers knew how important a fresh arm could be down the stretch.

The next night, Bankhead coasted to his 19th win with a 12–1 victory at Springfield, but the Dodgers had a rude awakening when they headed to their locker room at Pynchon Park after the game. Burglars had broken into the clubhouse during the game and ransacked the room, scattering clothes everywhere and stealing $150 from the pants pocket of J.J. Murphy, who was planning to send the money to his wife and new daughter. Campanis also had $29 stolen.

Springfield police never caught the culprits, but it seemingly was the only way the Dodgers would give up something easily.

Bird paid immediate dividends in his first start for his new team the next night, striking out 11 as the Dodgers beat Springfield, 9–6. Bartz drove in four runs on a two-run homer and two-run double while Hoak had another three hits as Nashua won its seventh straight.

As Nashua put the finishing touches on its 30th win in its past 40 games and the bus headed back east, little did the Dodgers know that in less than 24 hours they would see Bankhead's final pitching performance in a Nashua uniform.

Plus, they'd be taking part in the social event of the summer.

◆ ◆ ◆ ◆

About 3,500 people packed the aisles at Holman Stadium, clamoring for a better look, cameras poised and ready. But the event was a bit out of place in a baseball stadium.

Robert Ludwick and Dorothy Bickings were planning on marrying once his season with the Nashua Dodgers finally drew to a close. But word of the impending nuptials reached the ears of Mario Vagge, who knew he couldn't pass up an opportunity to stage the wedding of the year.

Vagge, the head of the Dodgers fan committee, thought it

would be a great opportunity to perform the ceremony at the ballpark—and maybe squeeze a few more fans through the turnstiles, despite the insistence of the Dodgers organization that "that wasn't the intention."

"Mario Vagge was an entrepreneur, and he was looking for something to happen," recalled Ludwick, a left-handed pitcher. "He got the idea that we should be married at home plate, so we agreed. We were going to get married after the season anyway, so we figured, why not?"

Team president Fred H. Dobens, also the publisher of *The Nashua Telegraph* at the time, went out of his way to set the record straight.

"The Dodgers did not plan this wedding and gave permission reluctantly only after the management was convinced that Ludwick did really want to be married at the ballpark," Dobens said. "The Dodgers haven't got to the point where they are running weddings as come-ons to attract crowds to our ballgames."

But for a ballplayer making less than $200 a month, there probably couldn't have been a better opportunity. The ceremony was scheduled to take place before a game against the Portland Pilots on Aug. 20, and merchants immediately began lining up to present the couple with gifts.

"Vagge told us he would take care of everything—and he did," Ludwick said.

Well before the ceremony took place, Ludwick was greeted by well-wishers everywhere he went. And once word got out that New England's first ballpark wedding would be taking place over on Amherst Street, tickets began to fly out the door at the Holman Stadium box office.

A picture in *The Nashua Telegraph* showed Ludwick and Bickings picking out wedding rings at Scott Jewelry in downtown Nashua, and 6-year-old Joan Vigneault, the daughter of

Mr. and Mrs. Lucien Vigneault of Lock Street, was selected to be flower girl at the ceremony.

Buzzie Bavasi, the business manager in Nashua in the team's first season in 1946, returned to the city with his wife, coming down from Montreal, where he was business manager of the Dodgers' Triple-A team.

So everything was in place for the 20-year-old Ludwick and his 19-year-old bride-to-be. A ceremony that was thought to be another two months away was suddenly upon them.

On their wedding day, the Dodgers were enjoying one of their best seasons in the team's three-year existence, and despite the fact that average attendance had dropped from the two previous years, there were usually plenty of familiar faces in the stands.

"You knew all the fans back then, many of them by name," Ludwick said. "If you won, they would come out to the ballpark. We had great fan support."

But on the evening of Aug. 20, the ballgame was secondary. A shiny automobile pulled onto the grass around third base and Ludwick, dressed in his Dodgers uniform, and his brother and best man, William, stepped out and walked toward home plate. Bickings, dressed in a white satin gown with a long train, was escorted by her brother, Herbert, and preceded by Doris Ludwick, Robert's sister, and Mrs. Harry Kirn, the bride's sister and matron of honor.

The Rev. Willis A. Porter of the First Baptist Church in Nashua performed the short ceremony, which began at 8:15 p.m. At the conclusion of the service, the newlyweds walked under an arch of baseball bats held up by Ludwick's teammates and, after a thunderous ovation, drove off to the reception at the Loyal Hall.

After the game, players from the Nashua and Portland teams and their wives attended the reception. The bakers of

Life Bread presented a five-tiered cake for the couple and a collection among fans at the game yielded $550. The Ludwicks were also presented with an array of gifts from Nashua-area merchants.

"As we look back, my wife doesn't really think that highly of it," admitted Ludwick, who said his wife certainly would have preferred the more traditional ceremony. "She still doesn't look at the wedding album."

But as unconventional as it was, the Ludwicks' wedding was something that was the talk of the town for years to come.

"He thought we should get married so he could take care of me," Dorothy Ludwick said, "but I've been taking care of him ever since."

◆ ◆ ◆ ◆

The evening was bittersweet for the Dodgers. While the players were enjoying the post-game reception following the Ludwicks' wedding and Nashua's 5–1 win over Portland, baseball reality set in when the players learned that Bankhead had been recalled to Triple-A St. Paul after winning his 20th game of the season.

The pitching-thin parent club wanted Bankhead throwing against stronger competition should they need him as Brooklyn chased the Cardinals and Braves down the stretch, and promised Nashua it would send a suitable replacement. Brooklyn considered Bankhead to be the only pitcher in its entire minor league system capable of making the jump to Triple-A.

In his Nashua finale, Bankhead struck out nine Pilots and walked six while scattering five hits.

While Bankhead was leaving town, the Brooklyn Dodgers were already thinking ahead to the 1949 season. William P. Loes, "the most sought-after rookie in the USA," according to

Stawasz, was signed by Nashua the day after Bankhead headed West.

In 1947, Loes, a high school phenom from Astoria, N.Y., was presented with most valuable player awards from both the *New York Journal American* and *New York World Telegram.* A graduate of Bryant High School, he pitched his team to the New York City championship, throwing four no-hitters in the 1948 season. In three seasons with the Bryant varsity, Loes compiled a 19–4 record.

"The transaction cost local management a considerable sum of money for the bonus player," Stawasz wrote, adding that Loes was also being pursued by the New York Giants and Boston Braves.

Loes, however, would not be coming any closer to Nashua. For the remainder of the season, the 6-foot-1 right-hander traveled with Brooklyn and pitched batting practice. He was scheduled to report to the Nashua Dodgers the following spring in Vero Beach, Fla., the new spring training home of the Dodgers organization.

Bankhead was leaving the Dodgers on solid footing, however. With a weekend sweep of Portland, combined with Lynn's 7–1 loss to Manchester, Nashua found itself in a first-place tie with the Red Sox. On Aug. 23, the Dodgers stood at 72–35, more wins than either the 1946 or '47 Dodgers had at the same point. In fact, Nashua had more wins than either the National League (Braves, 65) or American League (Cleveland Indians, 70) leaders.

A doubleheader sweep of Providence at Holman pushed Nashua to a half-game lead over Lynn and stretched the Dodgers' win streak to 10 games as a crowd of 2,336 showed up to see Max Patkin, the Clown Prince of Baseball, perform between games.

The next night, the win streak—and sole possession of first

place—was history. Providence beat Nashua, 11–10, in the first game of a doubleheader, but the Dodgers certainly made it interesting. Trailing 11–3 in their final at-bat, Nashua scored seven runs—powered by a Bartz grand slam—before falling short.

Word of Nashua's success was starting to generate interest down in the Big Apple, and Branch Rickey and Fresco Thompson, the director of the Dodgers' farm system, headed to Nashua to take in a couple of games. One of those games, though, drew a crowd of just 513 fans under threatening skies. And despite the team's winning ways, rumors persisted that Dodger fans were seeing the final days of the team's stay at Holman Stadium.

Eberly, however, called whispers that the team would be moved to Maine "completely unfounded." It was beginning to become a common mantra.

"I've never heard of any such proposal from Brooklyn," Eberly said. "I'll admit attendance has been disappointing at Nashua Dodgers games this year, but it's not basis enough to move the team out of Nashua."

Despite his protestations, however, the numbers were bleak. With fewer than 10 home games remaining, the Dodgers had drawn about 42,000. Eberly had hoped to draw 100,000 for the season. When all the numbers were counted, he'd have to settle for a lot less.

◆ ◆ ◆ ◆

As quickly as the Dodgers were able to enjoy the view atop the New England League standings, they found themselves looking back up at the Lynn Red Sox.

After Nashua pulled out a dramatic 3–2 win over the Springfield Cubs, it headed down to Lynn for a three-game series at Fraser Field. It was a two-team race, as Portland, which had remained in contention for most of the season, was beginning to fade. It was clear that the 1948 NEL pennant would be flying in either Nashua or Lynn.

Three days later, Lynn was back in control. Bartz drove in both runs in the Dodgers' 5–2 loss in the series opener, and Dick Nidds threw a six-hitter in the Saturday night game as Lynn blanked Nashua, 3–0. In the Sunday finale, Nashua jumped out to a 2–0 lead in the first inning off Lynn's Joe Tully, but was held to a single run on one hit over the next five innings and dropped a 10–7 decision. Lee, Cardinale and Murphy had two RBIs each, but Lynn had already built up an 8–2 lead before the Dodgers' bats answered.

The lone highlight of the weekend was Doc Alexson Day at Fraser Field. Friends and relatives from his nearby hometown of Ipswich made the short trip down Route 1 to honor the New England League's leading hitter. Boston Red Sox players Matt Batts—a Lynn alumnus—and Johnny Pesky were in attendance, as was Stuffy McInnis, a Gloucester, Mass., native and 19-year major league veteran who retired in 1927 and had taken Alexson under his wing, as well as Alexson's high school coach, Jim Burke.

The latest addition to the Dodgers' rotation, Leon Griffeth, made his debut in a Nashua uniform as the locals returned to familiar turf. His five-hitter paced the Dodgers to a 5–0 victory, a win that closed out August with Nashua three games behind Lynn.

Ah, but the excitement was just beginning.

Manchester gained a measure of revenge the next night with a 5–3 win over the Dodgers at Athletic Park, but it wasn't without fireworks. Both Murphy and Campanis were thrown out of the game, which the Dodgers played under protest after Campanis felt umpires blew a call on a stolen base in the seventh inning, one of six the Yankees had in the game. Two of those swipes were by league leader Frank Verdi, who notched his 62nd and 63rd steals of the season.

Nashua got back on track with a 10–6 victory over the reeling Pilots, who dropped their seventh straight game. Bird, in relief of Beres, got the win after entering the game with the Dodgers trailing, 6–3. Bartz continued his torrid hitting, belting his 38th double of the season and driving in three runs to push his RBI total to 98.

Portland again fell victim to the Dodgers the next night, and Pilots ace Kolosna hardly resembled the pitcher who had handcuffed Nashua three weeks earlier. The Dodgers pounded the sore-armed Kolosna for nine runs in $4^{2}/_{3}$ innings to chase him from the game.

Lynn, though, was showing no signs of letting up, winning its 11th straight game with an 8–2 victory over Manchester to lower the magic number for clinching the NEL pennant to one.

Alas, the Dodgers had one final chance, and Sept. 4–6 were probably dates Nashua fans had circled on their calendars several months ago: a three-game series against the Red Sox for all the marbles at Holman Stadium. But by virtue of Lynn's sweep of Nashua the previous weekend, there was no room for error. All Lynn had to do was win one game. One Nashua loss and the hated Red Sox would be celebrating their third straight NEL pennant on the Holman infield.

It was all Nashua in the series opener. Griffeth and Beres combined for a five-hitter and Russ Nelson and Cardinale drove in two runs each as the Dodgers rolled to a 9–0 victory. Nashua scored seven runs in the second inning off Lynn starter Rollie Schuster, handing the 18-game winner just his fourth loss of the season.

Nashua was within three games of the Red Sox with four

to play, including two more against Lynn. Dodgers fans could smell the pennant.

The optimism, however, lasted just 24 hours.

Nashua and Lynn completed nine innings with the score tied, 1–1. The Dodgers, though, were in a giving mood. After two Nashua errors and a Fred Hatfield steal of home, Nashua was looking at a 4–1 deficit heading into the bottom of the 10th inning.

Don Falling, who had shut the Dodgers down the week before, scattered five hits, but ran into trouble before yielding to Joe Tully, who induced Wally Rogers to bounce into a game-ending, pennant-clinching double play.

Sunday's 9–1 loss to Lynn was academic, as was the Dodgers' doubleheader sweep of Manchester on Labor Day to close out the regular season. Alexson's tie-breaking single in the bottom of the ninth of the second game—one of four RBIs the first baseman had in the game—allowed the Dodgers to pull out a 6–5 win.

Before the game, the Nashua fans presented each player with a wallet with a $100 bill inside. Bat boy Johnny Winn, batting practice catcher Leo Lavoie and clubhouse manager "Pop" Worthen were also given gifts.

In the end, Nashua had fallen one game short of winning the flag, finishing with an excellent .672 winning percentage (84–41). But there was hardly a reason to feel uneasy about the playoffs. In its two previous seasons, Nashua's professional baseball team had already proven that winning the regular season crown meant nothing. It's who's holding onto the Governor's Cup at the end of the New England League play-offs that really mattered.

The Dodgers had already won the first two championships of the reformed New England League. And as far as the team and its fans were concerned, it was time to make room in the trophy case for another.

◆ ◆ ◆ ◆

Despite its failure to win either of the first two Governor's Cup finals, everyone outside of Nashua figured Lynn had too much not to win it in 1948.

At the same time, not many league insiders were giving the Dodgers serious consideration.

"We weren't expected to win," Massar said. "But we were a close team—all the Dodgers teams were that way. And we knew we could win the Governor's Cup. That's all that mattered."

In the first round of the playoffs, the Dodgers played fourth-place Pawtucket (61–64), which finished a distant fourth, 24 games behind the Red Sox, 23 behind Nashua, while Lynn squared off against Portland.

Rather than go with Karl Morrison or Mike Quill, two pitchers who had been around the entire season, Campanis decided to give the ball to Bird, who went 3–1 down the stretch after coming over from Pawtucket.

Bird didn't disappoint against his old mates. The right-hander went the distance, surrendering just three hits, while Nashua made the most of its two hits off George Uhle in taking the opener, 3–1.

And while nobody seemed to get very comfortable against Uhle, Murphy did just fine. He had both of the Dodgers' hits, scored the second run on Alexson's sacrifice fly in the fourth inning, and knocked in the insurance run in the sixth.

Just 981 fans showed up at Holman the next night, but it didn't faze the Dodgers, who blasted the Slaters, 10–4, to take a 2–0 lead in the series. Morrison walked four Slaters in the first inning, though none scored. It would prove to be Pawtucket's best chance of taking control as Morrison settled down to scatter nine hits and just one more walk while striking out eight in going the distance.

Cardinale's two-run double highlighted the Dodgers' four-run third to break a 3–3 tie.

Three nights later, 2,000 fans showed up at McCoy Stadium to lend moral support in hopes the Slaters could climb back into the series. It didn't work.

Bill Samson shut down Pawtucket, 6–1, and the Dodgers eliminated the Slaters from the first round of the NEL playoffs for the third straight year. Murphy again was the hitting star with three RBIs (including a two-run double) and Nelson drove in a pair. Samson helped his own cause with an RBI single in the eighth.

The series Dodgers fans were anticipating materialized when Lynn beat Portland in the winner-take-all fifth game, 3–2, when Jim Argeros beat Pilots shortstop Americo Romello's throw home with the bases loaded to score the game-winning run in the ninth.

It was as if a Nashua-Lynn final was a foregone conclusion. Portland had played well all season before faltering down the stretch and then fell to the Red Sox in the semifinals. Pawtucket made the postseason only because there had to be four teams and proved to be a mere bump in the road for the Dodgers.

While the chill of another New England autumn enveloped the region, the two teams that had spent most of the season doing their best to knock each other's block off had finally reached the end of the road. The natural rivalry with Manchester paled in comparison to the outright disdain many Dodgers players had for Lynn.

And while Nashua was in the heart of Red Sox country, it was far from *Lynn* Red Sox country. Nashua's baseball faithful bled Dodger blue. Many fans knew there was a good chance they might someday see a few former Lynn ballplayers gracing Fenway Park, but they'd just as soon see them with heads bowed, watching silently as the Dodgers celebrated another New England League championship.

Preferably at Holman Stadium.

Some allegiances die hard; some never get a chance to get started.

◆ ◆ ◆ ◆

Back in 1946, the Lynn-Nashua rivalry got a healthy start when Red Sox manager Pip Kennedy spoiled a hard-fought Dodgers win by saying that Nashua never would have beaten Lynn "if it wasn't for those two niggers," referring to Roy Campanella and Don Newcombe. They also happened to be two of the most talented players in the league, but that didn't matter to Kennedy or, it seems, many of the players he managed.

General manager Buzzie Bavasi's tirade after the comment, in which he had to be physically restrained from attacking Kennedy, was just one of many displays of unity and support Bavasi and the Dodgers players showed for Campanella and Newcombe.

The teams finished 1–2 in 1946, and again in 1947, although the Dodgers won their second straight NEL championship by beating Manchester, which had knocked off Lynn in the first round of the playoffs.

In 1948, nothing had changed. When Labor Day rolled around, Lynn still held the upper hand over Nashua in the regular-season standings, and when the playoffs started, the teams were again on a collision course.

A quintessential example of the teams' distaste for each

other came in Game 1 of the NEL championship. Charlie Bird was quickly becoming the most valuable member of the Dodgers' pitching staff since arriving from Pawtucket. Bird tossed a six-hitter against Lynn at Fraser Field as the Dodgers won, 4–1.

Bird had frustrated Red Sox hitters all night, and in the eighth inning he struck out third baseman Fred Hatfield. Hatfield argued vehemently with the home plate umpire that Dodgers catcher J.J. Murphy had dropped the ball after Hatfield swung and missed. Murphy let Hatfield know he had indeed held onto the ball, and shoved it under Hatfield's nose to prove his point.

Hatfield erupted and before either of the player's teammates could reach home plate, Hatfield and Murphy traded a number of punches. Both players were ejected, and the bad blood that had been so prevalent in the rivalry again bubbled to the surface.

Alexson had a hand in all four Nashua runs, knocking in two with a double and a triple and scoring two others. It marked the fifth time in six playoff games that the Red Sox had been outhit.

The next night, it was the same old Dodger magic as Nashua improved to 5–0 in the playoffs with a 5–2 victory over Lynn before 2,171 fans at Fraser Field. It was Karl Morrison's turn to handcuff Lynn this time, scattering seven hits, while Bartz drove in two runs. Nashua stole five bases in the game, including a triple steal in the seventh, with Walt Rogers scoring.

Don Falling, whom the Dodgers had had so little success against during the regular season, got the loss.

Lynn finally snapped the Dodgers' unbeaten run through the playoffs with a 3–2 victory in Game 3 at Holman, doing all its scoring in the first inning off starter Mike Quill. Hatfield got a measure of revenge with a two-run homer and Dale Long hit a bomb over the centerfield fence as the Dodgers found themselves down 3–0 before even swinging a bat.

Nashua scored two runs in the third, but Lynn catcher Jim Argeros picked Bartz off first for the final out of the inning with a runner on third.

A sparse Holman crowd of 1,366 saw the Dodgers take a 3–1 lead in the series with a 6–2 victory in Game 4. Once again, Bird kept the Red Sox off balance in getting his second win of the series. Lynn touched him up for 10 hits and he only had two strikeouts, but his submarine style of pitching was one that baffled the Red Sox.

Bob Lee went 3-for-4 and drove in two runs with a two-run triple in the bottom of the first while Phil Cardinale had a two-run single in the eighth to give the Dodgers some breathing room.

Red Sox starter Rollie Schuster, who went 18–4 during the regular season, lasted just one-third of an inning as Nashua scored four runs.

The teams returned to Lynn for Game 5 with the Red Sox hoping that the friendlier confines would help them get back into the series. Instead, Fraser Field took on all the excitement of a funeral parlor.

Not to be outdone by Bird, Morrison threw the best game of any Dodgers pitcher in the playoffs, surrendering just two hits as Nashua claimed its third straight Governor's Cup with an 11–0 laugher. It was Morrison's second win of the series and third of the playoffs, while Falling again failed to fool the Dodgers.

After taking a 1–0 lead in the first inning, the Dodgers broke the game open with a three-run second inning and scored another in the third on a Murphy RBI single.

Nashua put the finishing touches on the Red Sox with

four runs in the eighth, utilizing four walks, two singles and a two-run double by Bartz.

By the middle of the afternoon the following day, Holman Stadium was silent. Campanis left town early that morning with his wife and two sons, headed home to Brooklyn to continue his duties as scout for the Brooklyn Dodgers football team as well as carry on work in the baseball offices.

Massachusetts residents Doc Alexson, J.J. Murphy and Joe Soskovich had also returned home. Alexson was looking forward to a fall of refereeing football games, while Murphy would take a little time off before beginning work for a meat distribution plant in Boston.

Walt Rogers was planning a trip to the White Mountains with his new bride before heading home.

En route to Detroit, Ted Bartz would stop by the Brooklyn team offices to be examined by doctors who were concerned about a heart murmur. Given the high regard he was held by the Brooklyn hierarchy, the team wanted to make sure Bartz was OK before sending him home for the winter. Tests showed no reason for concern.

Phil Cardinale, who batted .258 and drove in 58 runs during the regular season before becoming a vital part of the Dodgers' run through the playoffs, was given his unconditional release by the team.

Morrison was assigned to Greenville of the South Atlantic League while Rogers was recalled to Fort Worth. Griffeth was sent up to St. Paul of the American Association, replacing Dan Bankhead, who moved on to Brooklyn's top minor league affiliate in Montreal after going 4–0 after his recall from Nashua with three weeks left in the regular season.

◆ ◆ ◆ ◆

But while Nashua fans reveled in yet another championship, the numbers off the field weren't good. As the Dodgers prepared for the playoffs, the team had hoped the lukewarm reception it had received at the box office would get a hearty boost as the stakes increased. Instead, the hoped-for boon turned out to be a bust.

In four home playoff games, the team drew a total of only 6,379, an average of 1,595 fans. Attendance on the road was even worse. In one game at Pawtucket and three games at Lynn, 5,224 fans went through the turnstiles, just 1,306 per game.

As a result, playoff shares were abysmal. As the winning team, Nashua earned 60 percent of the $797.64 in gate receipts, or $478.64. Given the full 20 playoff shares, each member of the Dodgers received the grand total of $23.93. Many ballplayers would be quick to point out that they weren't in it for the money, but the playoff bonuses were hardly more than chump change.

Red Sox players were even worse off, taking home just $15.95 each.

For the season, Nashua drew 63,382, an average of slightly more than 1,000 fans per game. The numbers paled in comparison to those from 1946 (1,445) and were not much better than 1947 (1,124) and detailed a disturbing trend, not only in Nashua, but across the New England League: Baseball fans were making fewer trips to the ballpark.

It was a situation that troubled Eberly, who was ultimately responsible for the team's bottom line. With television becoming more popular and fans finding alternative means to spend their hard-earned money, coupled with a disturbing and frightening downturn in the economy—especially in the Northeast—there were plenty of baseball people worried about the future of minor league baseball.

The Nashua Dodgers had gone home champions after each of the three seasons since the New England League was reincarnated in 1946. But the joy on the field was overshadowed by the worry off it. Neither the Dodgers nor the other teams in the league could survive if the attendance numbers continued to plummet. Portland, which teetered on extinction after a horrible first season two years before, led the NEL in attendance at 117,606. Springfield, in its first season in the league, was at 95,406. But there was a huge dropoff from there to Nashua's 63,382. Pawtucket (60,432), Manchester (50,664) and Lynn (49,088) had their own troubles at the gate, while Providence (28,170) and Fall River (22,589)—which finished 40 and 47 games out of first place, respectively—were close to bankruptcy.

To say that league executives were concerned with what the 1949 season would bring would be an understatement. The Dodgers' fortunes in Nashua were about to fall prey to forces well beyond the team's control.

1949:
End of the Innocence

AT A TIME WHEN THE regional economy was already reeling, the last thing anyone wanted to hear was more bad news.
By 1948, Nashua's fortunes were deeply entwined in the textile industry, a company town with a number of manufacturers producing products like blankets, shoes and sheets.

In fact, much of the city's industrial base was dependent
on the mills of the Nashua Manufacturing Co., and many in
the city became increasingly nervous as company after company headed South in search of more advanced machinery,
less expensive overhead—and cheaper, non-unionized labor.

In the years before World War II, many textile manufacturers had already begun consolidating operations and moving others completely out of the area. The onset of the war
and the resulting demand for textile goods, however, provided a temporary reprieve from the closings.

Nashua was not alone in this economic quandary. Mills in
Manchester, Lowell and Lawrence were closing and thou-

sands of workers without training in any other form of work found themselves desperately seeking means of employment.

City officials had hoped that Textron's purchase of the struggling Nashua Manufacturing Co. in 1945 would somehow help the economy rebound. But by mid-1947, it was apparent to Textron officials that the Nashua operations hadn't turned out to be as profitable as first thought, and company founder Royal Little stressed that changes would have to be made if the mills were to remain in operation.

The "Nashua Plan" was introduced, in which 1,500 workers, regardless of their seniority, would be laid off, and others would have their wages decreased while their workloads increased. Additionally, Textron asked the city for immediate tax cuts to help bring the company's books back in line.

But before the reorganization could be orchestrated, Textron dropped the real bombshell. On Sept. 13, 1948, the textile manufacturers announced that after 125 years of operations, the Nashua mills would be closed. The $1 million upgrade promised in return for the union's agreement to the layoffs was withdrawn and the remaining 3,600 workers at the Textron facilities—about one quarter of Nashua's workforce—soon found themselves out on the street.

Making the situation more of a boiling point was word that Textron, at the same time it was closing its operations in the Northeast, was actually following through with a $12 million expansion of many of its facilities in the South.

The city's workers erupted in rage. They gathered outside the gates of the factories and burned Little in effigy, skewering the smoldering mass on the wrought iron fence.

Then the reality of the situation began to set in.

"There was a look in the eyes of the people one passed on the street that reminded one of the way people looked in the

1930s (during the Great Depression)," the Rev. Edward Cahill, then-minister of the Unitarian Church, was quoted as saying in *The Nashua Telegraph*.

City and state government officials did not back down easily and urged an inquiry by the N.H. Senate Small Business Committee. Two days of hearings between company and union officials were held in Nashua in late September by a subcommittee of the Committee on Interstate and Foreign Commerce. Union officials portrayed Little as a reckless capitalist, another opportunist interested in nothing but the bottom line as he attempted to expand his textile empire.

For his part, Little adamantly defended his decision to close Textron, although he admitted that the mills were indeed turning a profit. He felt that in the years to come, however, the Nashua operations would become less and less profitable, and he was simply getting out before he suffered huge losses.

As part of an agreement, Textron's sheet manufacturing facility at the Jackson Mill would retain 1,000 jobs and remain open at least until December 1951, but the blanket manufacturing operations would only be maintained for another three months, until Dec. 31, 1948.

The city swung into action, forming the Nashua New Hampshire Foundation, and eventually bought 2.5 million square feet of mill space from Little for $500,000. The foundation, bolstered by an all-out publicity blitz by the Chamber of Commerce, began wooing new industries to the city. Within six years, many of the city's abandoned structures were beginning to fill with a more diverse selection of industrial clientele.

Before that successful economic upturn would be realized, however, there were plenty of people worried about having enough money to put meals on the table—never mind going to a ballgame.

◆ ◆ ◆ ◆

Despite the shaky financial ground on which many New England League teams ended the 1948 season—including the Manchester Yankees, who had finished $18,000 in the red—the eternal optimism of baseball nonetheless brought high hopes for the coming season.

One day after Eberly made it clear that the 1949 Dodgers would not have a player/manager at the helm, as the previous three teams had, the team announced that Greg Mulleavy, a 44-year-old resident of Jamestown, N.Y., would be the team's skipper.

Mulleavy came to Nashua with nine years of managerial experience. In his fourth year with the Brooklyn organization, Mulleavy was highly recommended by Rickey and many others in Dodgers management after leading Greenville to the South Atlantic League championship in 1948 after the team finished third in the regular season.

Mulleavy knew all too well the difficulty of fighting one's way through the minors, withstanding long bus rides and subpar playing fields, but he never lost focus. He began his professional career in 1927 as an infielder with Petersburg of the Virginia League and made stops at Raleigh, N.C., San Antonio, Decatur, Ill., and Toledo before finally making it to the majors with the Chicago White Sox in 1930.

He appeared in 77 games in his rookie season, batting .263 with 14 doubles and five triples while driving in 28 runs and scoring 27. The White Sox (62–92) were a terrible team, finishing 40 games behind the pennant-winning Philadelphia

Athletics, but 10 games ahead of the last-place Red Sox (52–102).

Mulleavy's dreams of remaining in the majors—at least with the White Sox—would be short-lived, however, with the arrival of future Hall-of-Fame shortstop Luke Appling. Mulleavy spent most of the 1931 season at Toledo, appeared in one game with the White Sox in 1932 after being called up from Triple-A Oakland, and played one game for the Boston Red Sox in 1933 after a recall from Triple-A Buffalo. He returned to Buffalo in 1934 and remained there until 1940.

Mulleavy began his managerial career in 1941 and won two pennants and a league championship with Jamestown of the Class D Pony League before taking over at Buffalo in 1943. He returned to the Pony League in 1944 and managed Lockport, N.Y., for two seasons before joining the Dodgers organization.

On Feb. 15, Eberly met with members of the Nashua Kiwanis Club to discuss the impact of television on baseball. Major league officials envisioned the new medium attracting millions of new fans to the game, but Eberly was among many worried that television would have a huge negative impact on the minor leagues, costing them tens of thousands of fans who would just as soon enjoy watching a ballgame—free of charge—in the comfort of their own living room. Minor league officials, who were protected against other teams moving into their region by baseball's territorial rights clause, could not get major league officials to maintain this provision regarding television broadcasts.

The Radio Corporation of America, which owned NBC, had begun experimental telecasts into 150 New York homes in 1936 and technology progressed slowly before the onset of World War II. Television broadcasting was suspended when the United States entered the war and remained that way until the war ended in 1945.

Bolstered by an economic resurgence brought on by a war victory, Americans began joining the television boom in earnest. By 1951, America's broadcasting companies would extend their reach from coast to coast and television stations began popping up all over the country. There may have been fewer than 10,000 television sets in America in 1945, but by 1950, there were about six million sets in use; 10 years later, that number jumped tenfold to about 60 million. America's fascination with the television was well under way.

Television's effect on baseball was immediately felt in the New York metropolitan area. For those fans who either had no means of getting to the ballpark or couldn't afford to go to many games, television's free access was a godsend. In the mid-'50s, Newark and Jersey City of the International League suffered huge financial losses at the gate as the result of regular broadcasts of Yankees, Giants and Dodgers games.

"Television was a definite rival for fans for all of us in the minor leagues," Eberly said. "But the closing of the textile mills played a huge role. I was berated because someone asked me about the situation and I thought it deserved an honest answer. When they closed those textile mills, I knew that was bad news. I knew we were in trouble."

The team immediately swung into action, freezing the price of tickets at 80 cents for adults and 30 cents for children. A 10-game ticket package cost $7.25, a savings of 75 cents, and would admit fans to any 10 regular-season games.

Eberly, admitting the move was made to stimulate lagging ticket sales, estimated that 138,000 paid admissions were necessary to meet the team's normal operating budget, about $70,000 for the season. The team, though, got just a 65 percent cut—52 cents—from the 80-cent admission charge.

From every ticket sold, the New England League took 5 cents, the visiting team received 10 cents, and 13 cents was set aside to pay taxes.

Meanwhile, the Nashua Dodgers were preparing to open spring training camp at Vero Beach, Fla. Among the 31 players expected, seven were beginning their first season of organized baseball. One of those was highly touted left-hander Billy Loes, the bonus baby the Brooklyn Dodgers discovered in their own backyard. Another pitcher drawing raves was a lefty from Norristown, Pa., named Thomas Lasorda, who had signed a contract with Nashua in the offseason.

"If Lasorda does as well as the two boys we drafted last year (Ted Bartz and Doc Alexson, who finished 1–2 in the NEL batting race), he'll be quite a pitcher," Eberly said.

◆ ◆ ◆ ◆

As player contracts slowly filtered back to Eberly's office and the start of spring training approached, excitement began to build. On Feb. 24, *The Nashua Telegraph* published the New England League schedule, and right there in the top corner was the season opener: Lynn Tigers vs. Nashua Dodgers, April 30, at Holman Stadium. Lynn had indeed changed affiliations, parting company with the Red Sox and hooking up with the Detroit Tigers. But a familiar face would be calling the shots at Fraser Field: Thomas "Pip" Kennedy, a man Dodgers fans had taken a measurable dislike to.

A few other recognizable baseball names took over managerial posts in the league. Wally Berger, the former home run king for the Boston Braves (1930–37), who also played for Cincinnati and the New York Giants, took over the Manchester Yankees, replacing Tom Padden. Dick Porter, who played in the Cleveland Indians and Red Sox systems, was named the Fall River Indians' manager while James A. "Ripper" Collins, a first baseman who led the National League in home runs (35) and slugging percentage (.615) in 1934 while a member of the famed Gashouse Gang St. Louis Cardinals, was the new Pawtucket manager.

Lamar A. "Skeeter" Newsome, who spent 12 years in the majors with the Philadelphia Athletics, Red Sox and Philadelphia Phillies, and played the 1948 season with Seattle of the Pacific Coast League, took over in Portland.

The only returning manager was Bob Peterson, whose Springfield Indians finished well into the second division with a 52–74 record (33½ games behind pennant-winning Lynn) but was second in the league in attendance (95,406).

As spring training got under way in Vero Beach, Fla., with Nashua, Sheboygan, Wisc., Geneva, N.Y., and Cambridge, Md., the last of the Brooklyn affiliates to report to camp, word began to filter north that the Dodgers might have a pretty darn good ballclub.

Mulleavy was especially fond of what he was seeing of his young pitching staff. In a short dispatch to Eberly, Mulleavy spoke of the talents of pitchers Marion Fricano, Bob Ludwick, Alton Gilbert and Norman Gosselin.

"But our brightest prospect is Billy Loes," Mulleavy added. "He's living up to press notices."

Another pitcher gaining attention in Florida was Pete Nicolas, a high school teammate of Loes'. But while Loes was handling the bulk of the pitching duties at Bryant High School—throwing five no-hitters in his senior season—Nicolas had to be content playing right field. He also batted .414 for the season.

It was apparent from the start that Brooklyn had big plans for the 18-year-old Loes. After nearly losing the hometown boy when he was courted by the Cleveland Indians before signing with Brooklyn for a $25,000 bonus, he began showing signs in spring training that he could be the dominant pitcher the team had envisioned.

His numbers during his senior season of high school were staggering. He won 15 straight games, including nine by shutout. He struck out 125 batters, an average of 13 per game, while walking just 21. The cocky right-hander predicted he'd throw a no-hitter in his final high school game—then went out and did it.

After graduating from high school, Loes was asked to pitch against a semi-pro team to see how he'd fare against non-high school competition. He threw a four-hitter and struck out 10 in a 4–1 victory. With scouts from nearly every major league club in the stands, the Dodgers soon realized they'd have to dig deep into their pockets if they were to keep Loes close to home.

In his first spring training with a big-league club, Loes drew rave reviews.

"His biggest attribute is his fine control," Brooklyn scout Eddie McCarrick said. "He seldom gets rattled, and as a result is always able to find the strike zone when the going gets tough. That gives him a big jump on the other rookie hurlers, most of whom are inclined to be wild."

Mulleavy thought so highly of Loes that just days into camp he reportedly had already decided to make Loes Nashua's opening day starter.

The Dodgers were expected to arrive via train at Boston's South Station on April 21, with the players reaching Nashua later that evening and checking into the Kernwood Hotel. On April 19, team officials expressed satisfaction that close to 2,500 tickets had already been sold for the April 30 season opener.

Around the same time, the team received word that it

might be getting another "bonus baby," likely to join the team once it arrived in town. The Brooklyn front office wasn't letting on who it was, but Eberly no doubt was excited about the effect another top-notch prospect might have on the gate.

A day later, Eberly received word that Wayne Belardi, an 18-year-old first baseman from San Jose, Calif., would join the team. Belardi, one of the most sought-after prospects on the West Coast, had received a $15,000 bonus for signing with Santa Barbara, the Dodgers' Class C affiliate in the California League.

Belardi had been working out with Triple-A Montreal during spring training and apparently had won the starting job, but Brooklyn didn't want to rush him, so he was sent to Newport News. The solid-hitting, slick-fielding prospect also possessed good speed (7.0 seconds in 60-yard dash), and at 6-foot-1, 185 pounds, had already started to fill out.

Major League Baseball's rules stated that "bonus baby" signees had to be placed on the major league roster by the start of the next season or the players would be subjected to a minor league draft. It presented a difficult decision for many teams to make: Do you hope that your prospect has a sub-par season and teams pass on the chance of signing him away, giving you the opportunity to "hide" him in the minors? Or do you set aside a roster spot for a player who may not see a lot of action, essentially limiting your manager's flexibility and possibly costing a valuable role player a major league job?

Whatever the decision teams made, the player was often caught in the middle, and the "bonus babies" hardly needed any extra pressure to play well. Nevertheless, Belardi's delayed arrival in Nashua saved him from seeing a Telegraph headline touting a most improbable comparison: "Another DiMaggio?"

Mulleavy, though, considered one of the top assessors of

talent in the Brooklyn organization, felt Belardi was going to show plenty of promise.

"They just can't get that ball by him when he's got a bat in his hands," he said.

The team arrived at Nashua's Union Station with 12 pitchers, five infielders, three outfielders and two catchers, and Mulleavy, though acknowledging the team was inexperienced, was excited about the team's prospects.

"We're a very young ballclub, probably the youngest in the league," the manager said. "That means a lack of experience. But don't forget these boys received the same training at Vero Beach that the major league and Triple-A clubs received, and that's going to show during the season."

In their annual exhibition against the semi-pro New England Hoboes, the Dodgers rolled to an 11–1 victory, banging out 12 hits and drawing 11 walks. Loes scattered three hits and four walks while striking out six in seven innings or work.

Shortstop Bob Kehoe went 4-for-5 with two RBIs, outfielder Don Taylor had a triple and double and three RBIs while shortstop Billy Hunter drove in two runs. Nashua also stole nine bases, with Hunter and outfielder Johnny Zack getting three each and Kehoe swiping two.

The Dodgers played two more exhibition games in preparation for the season opener, falling to Pawtucket, 5–4, and being blanked by Manchester, 5–0. Nashua was held to just three hits in the game against the Yankees, but one of those was by newly arrived outfielder Gino Cimoli, who was optioned to Nashua from Santa Barbara and became the third "bonus baby" on the Nashua roster. Cimoli's signing bonus of $10,000 meant the Dodgers had three players with $50,000 bankrolled between them before ever getting a taste of pro ball.

◆ ◆ ◆ ◆

On opening night, 2,324 fans streamed through the turn-stiles to see the Dodgers begin their fourth season in the New England League. The crowd was smaller than those at the openers in each of the past three seasons, but the team was nonetheless satisfied with the pre-sale of more than 2,000 tickets to the game.

The Dodgers, like most every other team in the New England League—or much of minor league baseball, for that matter—had watched agonizingly as its fan base had shrunk noticeably, and team and civic leaders decided to get together and make a concerted effort to renew interest in the team.

During a high-profile meeting at the Laton Hotel while the team was in the midst of spring training, officials devised a promotion called "King of the Fans," a program in which the most die-hard Dodgers fan would be recognized for their support. That most arduous supporter would arrive for the season opener via helicopter and be presented with a season pass for admission to all of the Dodgers' home games.

One of the early favorites in the contest was Earle L. Williams Jr., a clerk at Rice's Drug Store on Main Street. Chosen to represent the Knights of Columbus, Williams lived in the shadows of Holman Stadium, on Concord Street, and kept detailed records and statistics of every one of the Dodgers' home games over the previous three seasons.

It would be 12-year-old Jimmy Hogan who would be treated like royalty that Saturday night, however. There was no arrival by helicopter. In fact, the "King of the Fans" was late for his own coronation, delaying both the ceremony planned beforehand and the game.

Struggling to keep the crown level on his head, Hogan finally took the mound to the cheers of the crowd. He threw out the first pitch to J.J. Murphy, a fan favorite who had signed a contract to return to Nashua only days earlier, and collected his season ticket from Eberly.

Fans soon saw what they might be able to expect from two of Nashua's best ballplayers. Loes started on the mound and went the distance in the Dodgers' 7–2 victory over Lynn. The 19-year-old scattered seven hits and struck out four while walking just one. He got his first professional hit in the fourth inning.

The play of the night in a lopsided Nashua win, however, turned out to be a defensive gem. When a deep fly ball headed toward Cimoli in right field, the Tigers' Bill Cliggott figured he'd move up an extra 90 feet and put himself in better scoring position at third base. He toed second base and bolted as soon as he saw the ball enter Cimoli's glove.

With each stride he moved closer to Nashua third baseman Bob Kehoe, who was straddling the bag. But when Cliggott got within 10 feet of the bag, Cimoli's throw, estimated to be from a distance of 300 feet, popped into Kehoe's mitt at chest level—without touching the ground. Kehoe's snap tag nailed Cliggott, who could only look up at his manager, Pip Kennedy, shaking his head in the third-base coaching box.

"That was a big stadium," Cimoli said of Holman. "I remember the fence they had out there, I went right through it one game that year.

"I was just 18 years old. I didn't know what to expect. All I know is we were doing what we loved—playing baseball. After the first 30 or 40 games, we knew we had a hell of a team."

The next night, at Lynn's Fraser Field, another pitcher took his turn dominating hitters. Marion Fricano, who like second baseman Bobby Brown hailed from a small town in upstate New York, also threw a seven-hitter, striking out four and walking five, losing the shutout in the bottom of the ninth, but still leading the Dodgers to a 6–1 win over the Tigers.

Kehoe drove in three runs for Nashua, which also got its first home run of the season, a 400-foot shot by Murphy.

Nashua would beat Springfield twice and win its first four games before the Cubs would defeat the Dodgers, 9–1. Loes got hammered in his second pro start, giving up four hits and four runs in the first inning without getting an out.

On May 7, it was Belardi's turn to prove his worth. With two men on in the first inning, the smooth-swinging first baseman roped a ball into the right field corner and beat a path around the bases, not stopping until he crashed into Lynn catcher Don Griffin and knocked the ball loose for an inside-the-park three-run homer.

In the seventh, Belardi hit a 400-foot homer that also scored Billy Hunter, who had just hit his second double of the game after starting the season in a 1-for-22 funk.

Belardi's offensive prowess stole the thunder from Fricano, who was stellar in his second start of the season, throwing a six-hitter with three strikeouts in the Dodgers' 5–1 win over the Tigers.

After the first 10 games, Nashua was sitting atop the NEL standings with an 8–2 mark. Cimoli was hitting .394 while Taylor was batting .368. Everything was coming together on the field for the Nashua Dodgers, but the crowds at Holman Stadium were noticeably smaller. Nothing like the minuscule crowds showing up in Fall River and Providence, but certainly small enough to start making Eberly feel a bit uneasy.

◆ ◆ ◆ ◆

No one could dispute that Billy Loes had an uncanny ability to pitch a baseball. Certainly Mulleavy knew every time

Loes got the ball, he could pretty much count on a solid effort that usually resulted in a Dodgers win.

But Loes was loud, brash and boisterous, always seeming to go out of his way to impress his teammates. Aside from his high school buddy, Nicolis, nobody was really able to get too close to him. And as the Dodgers edged closer to the May 30 cut-down date, when teams would have to pare their rosters to 19 players, the little-used Nicolis—who many surmised was in Nashua simply to keep Loes company—was released. He finished his career in Nashua with just three innings pitched and a 12.00 earned run average.

Like most ballplayers, Loes was very superstitious and had a peculiar habit once he returned to the dugout after pitching.

"After every inning, he came into the dugout and had to be the third person from the left side sitting on the bench," recalled pitcher Norbert "Nob" Habel. "If you were sitting there talking to someone, he'd squeeze in right between you if it meant him sitting where he had to be."

Billy Hunter recalled a daredevil trip over to Holman Stadium in Loes' new Pontiac, one he purchased with part of his signing bonus.

"He was kind of crazy," Hunter remembered. "He gave me a ride over to the park and he was going up (Library Hill) to the top and he was stuck behind this truck that he obviously thought was going too slow. So he just went right around it. He had no idea if a car was coming the other way—he couldn't see. I wonder what would have happened to us if there was a car coming the other way.

"Anyway, he got around the truck and as soon as he got (on Amherst Street) I yelled at him to pull over. I got out and walked the rest of the way to the park. I never got into a car with him driving again."

Pitcher Bill Mosser, who joined the team in June, recalled a similar story.

"He picked us up in that car and he just scooted right by the park," Mosser said. "He was flying down the street. He was quite a character. Footloose and fancy-free."

The purchase of that new car early in the season was a classic Loes tale.

Not long after arriving in Nashua, Loes strode into the lobby of the Kernwood Hotel late one morning and, spying a few teammates lounging around, invited them to walk downtown to the Pontiac dealership. With nothing better to do, three or four of them tagged along.

Upon reaching the showroom, the group hardly mustered more than a passing glance from a handful of salesmen, who were more concerned that the group, clad in white T-shirts and chinos, might scare legitimate customers off. Loes sauntered around the showroom, checking out various models, while his teammates waited. Finally, after about 20 minutes, a salesman made his way over to offer assistance.

"I want to buy a car; this one right here," Loes said.

The salesman, smelling a nice commission, began to sweet-talk Loes about the features of the car, how he'd look good behind the wheel, and the many advantages of having the freedom to go anywhere he wanted.

After Loes showed a lukewarm response, the salesman began going over the various financing plans at Loes' disposal, but the pitcher cut the salesman short and uttered the words any salesman likes to hear. "I'll be paying cash for it."

"From that point on everything was, 'Yes, Mr. Loes. Will there be anything else, Mr. Loes?' " said Kehoe, one of those who accompanied Loes.

Faster than any 18-year-old should have been able to spend a couple thousand dollars, Loes counted out the money into the salesman's hands. After taking the money to the safe, the salesman returned with the keys to the new car, dangling them in front of Loes with an ear-to-ear grin.

Loes waved him off.

"Don't give me the keys," Loes said, in his thick Brooklyn accent, "I don't know how to drive."

"Billy Loes," Kehoe said, "was a crackpot."

◆ ◆ ◆ ◆

In the late evening hours of June 1, Loes, the cocky, confident, "crackpot" pitcher, was putting the finishing touches on his first professional no-hitter. Of the three no-hitters thrown by Nashua Dodgers pitchers in the franchise's four-year existence, though, Loes was the first to go nine innings.

Loes, who threw seven no-hitters as a schoolboy, was nothing short of spectacular, striking out 13 and walking just three as Nashua beat the Fall River Indians, 2–0. Only one batter got as far as second base: Paul Hart, who had walked and advanced on a passed ball.

The only run Loes would need came on an RBI double by outfielder Joe Riolo, playing in his fourth and final game for the Dodgers. Riolo, whose hit knocked in Cimoli in the second inning, left immediately after the game for Danville, Ill., as an emergency replacement for Brooklyn's other Class B team. Belardi added a solo homer in the seventh for an insurance run.

During the game, Cimoli didn't realize that Loes had a no-hitter going, and kept asking his teammates if it were true. Hardly willing to be held responsible for jinxing Loes' effort, outfielder Norm Postolese refused to answer Cimoli each time his outfield mate asked if Loes had given up a hit. At times, Postolose even walked away to avoid the question.

Any joy on the field, however, was beginning to be tempered on the business front. League president Claude Davidson called an emergency meeting for team representatives in Boston, with rumors flying that the Providence franchise was on the verge of folding.

"The Providence situation is serious," read a dispatch sent by Davidson to the league's general managers.

The NEL then announced it had taken over the Providence franchise after meeting with the team's stockholders and determining that the club was unable to meet its payroll. Davidson, acting on the instructions of the league's board of directors, assured the players that their salaries would be guaranteed by the NEL.

On June 10, just three days after Joe Pullano had taken over for Frank Pytlak as Providence manager, the NEL's board of directors issued an ultimatum, giving Providence four days to right the ship. Hopes of a solution were bolstered by word that the Philadelphia A's, St. Louis Cardinals and Cleveland Indians were each looking to secure a Class B affiliate. Regardless of the outcome, though, the Grays were not allowed to play another game at Cranston Stadium, their home field. If the franchise did survive, the Grays would play its home games in a new stadium being built in East Providence. The team's next two games, in fact, were scheduled to be moved to Pawtucket's McCoy Stadium.

Several days later, Davidson announced that the Providence franchise would remain in the league only if the city could provide a ballpark for the team within the city limits. The Athletics, at that point the only team still interested in acquiring the franchise, said they would step away from an affiliation if a park wasn't provided.

On June 21, the roof fell in. The New England League announced that Providence was being dropped from the league, with the NEL proceeding as a seven-team circuit. Each member of the Grays was pronounced a free agent, eligible to play for any other team in the league or elsewhere.

In Lynn, attendance problems were actually worse than in Providence, where only 7,305 fans had attended the first 25 games. But Tigers management reportedly was intent on finishing the season in Lynn before considering a move to the Lewiston-Auburn area of Maine if the New England League returned in 1950.

Things weren't much better in Fall River or Manchester. With a faltering textile economy handcuffing both mill cities and fans getting better—and free—access to their favorite major league teams through radio and television broadcasts, the death knell for struggling franchises was an inferior product on the field. It simply gave fans one more reason to stay away from the ballpark.

On June 20, *The Nashua Telegraph* sports editor Frank Stawasz offered the first convincing evidence that the Dodgers were beginning to get caught in the economic pinch.

> *Some folks in town think the 1949 Dodgers are the best team to represent Nashua in Class B baseball," he wrote. "Yet a glance at the attendance figures has us wondering if they'll be returning here come 1950.*
>
> *It takes a lot of money to field a minor league team, and why should the parent organization, the Brooklyn Dodgers, take a whaling at the box office when they can find many other cities eager to take over?*
>
> *Whether the Dodgers return here next season or not will be determined to a great extent on attendance from now until the Fourth (of July).*

Nashua had drawn a total of 10,000 for a three-game series against the Springfield Cubs that week, but two days after Stawasz's column appeared, just 585 fans attended the Dodgers' 6–2 win over Fall River. Through June 19, the Dodgers were averaging just 915 fans per game, compared to the league average of 1,137 — a number that also included the woeful attendance averages in Providence and Fall River.

On June 23, the Dodgers beat Pawtucket, 7–3, to snap the Slaters' 11-game win streak and forge a virtual tie atop the NEL standings, Nashua with a 37–15 record, Pawtucket with a 38–16 mark. It was already turning into a two-team race, with Springfield a distant third, nine games back.

Or so it seemed.

◆ ◆ ◆ ◆

Branch Rickey, whose fiscal conservatism was rivaled only by his rigid moral standards, was a bottom-line businessman. His decision in 1946 to recruit Jackie Robinson to eliminate baseball's racial barrier was at least partially motivated by economics: Rickey saw the opportunity to attract a vast, untapped legion of black baseball fans who up to that point hadn't had a reason to attend major league baseball games.

His reputation for hard-line negotiations of player contracts was legendary. More than one player left Rickey's office questioning his own baseball talent. His invention of the farm system when he was with the St. Louis Cardinals in the 1930s was an unabashed attempt to develop players who, as they rose through the ranks, were paid on a scale set by Rickey.

When the more talented players like future Hall-of-Famer Enos Slaughter did reach the major leagues, Rickey held the trump card, thanks to the iron-clad reserve clause. He didn't have to get into of a bidding war with other teams for their services because they were already Cardinals property. Rickey could pay them what he wanted to pay them or they wouldn't be playing professional baseball.

As Bill Eberly sat in his cramped and primitive Holman Stadium office and pored over the team ledger, he saw the same bottom line Rickey did—and it was written in red ink.

"You always had the feeling you should be doing something to get fans back into the ballpark," Eberly said. "It was difficult for all of those talented prospects to see there really wasn't anybody in the ballpark. It was discouraging for anyone who can run, hit and throw the ball 90 mph to look up in the stands and see no one there."

Even with Stawasz acting as Eberly's mouthpiece in that June 20 newspaper article, essentially telling Nashua baseball fans that if they didn't come out and support the team they could be looking at a summer without professional baseball the following year, the Fourth of July came and went with hardly a ripple of improvement in attendance figures at Holman Stadium.

Brooklyn front office personnel, namely Rickey and minor league director Fresco Thompson, had made it clear to Eberly that if there wasn't a marked improvement in attendance and interest in the Nashua club—and a resulting fiscal upturn—the wrecking ball might swing northward.

The wait was a short one.

On July 2, the Brooklyn organization, concerned with the economic struggles not only of its own New England League franchise but the entire league, began dismantling the most talented Dodgers team in its four years in Nashua.

The telephone call Eberly was expecting arrived as the Dodgers were about to embark on a road trip to Portland for a series against the Pilots.

"We're going to start sending these guys on," Thompson told Eberly in a brief conversation.

Gino Cimoli was sitting on the bus in the Holman Stadium parking lot when Eberly climbed the steps and called him off.

"You're going to Montreal," Eberly told Cimoli, who quickly packed his belongings and headed to Nashua's Union Station. He made his Triple-A debut the next night, playing both games of the Royals' doubleheader in Buffalo.

The Dodgers, undoubtedly still reeling from Cimoli's abrupt departure, were shelled in their first two games at Portland, watching the Pilots score seven runs in the fourth inning en route to a 10–6 win in the series opener, and falling behind 8–0 in an eventual 12–2 pummeling the following night.

Nashua avoided a sweep by banging out 17 hits in an 11–7 victory in the series finale.

Back home, while Eberly was struggling to keep things on an even keel in Nashua, he was also entrusted by Davidson with devising a revised league schedule after Providence ceased operations and rumors continued to swirl that Fall River was about to pull the plug. Eberly's solution called for the season to be divided into halves, with the first half ending on July 8. After the second half, the Governor's Cup playoffs would include the four teams with the best overall records.

Fall River hadn't formally announced its departure from the New England League, but all indications were that owner Joe Madowsky was planning to do exactly that. The Indians hadn't turned a profit since 1946, and with Lynn officials already saying the Tigers wouldn't field a team next season unless they moved operations to Maine, the league was sputtering. Nashua was plodding through its worst season by far at the gate and "Manchester has been on the verge of quitting the league for several seasons now," Stawasz wrote on July 5.

A few days later, Madowsky announced that Fall River would stay in the league after he received assurances from two major league teams that would provide players to the Indians.

But in Nashua, the upheaval continued when Brooklyn dropped another bomb, shipping Loes off to Double-A Fort Worth in a four-pitcher transaction that also included promoting promising prospect Carl Erskine to Brooklyn. Loes finished his Nashua career with an 11–3 record and 2.80 ERA. He gave up just 85 hits in 122 innings pitched while striking out 95. Even though there were nearly two months remaining in the regular season when he was promoted, Loes, who would go on to pitch for 11 years in the major leagues, would lead the New England League with four shutouts.

To make matters worse, word around the clubhouse was that Belardi wouldn't be around much longer, either.

"When the Fourth of July rolled around and there wasn't much improvement (in attendance), you knew that something was going to happen," Eberly said. "It's one of those businesses where you can't control your own destiny. You're at the mercy of the people paying the bills. And the lack of player continuity was justified because we weren't filling the ballpark. Why have all of these promising players playing in a stadium where no one was coming to see them play?"

Unlike the cases of Cimoli and Loes, the Nashua Dodgers got a bit of advance notice on the imminent departure of Belardi. On July 11, the team announced Belardi, the New England League's leading home run hitter, would soon be moving on to Greenville of the Class A South Atlantic League.

Two nights later, Belardi cracked his 15th homer of the season in his final home game, a 10–1 victory over Springfield, which also included the first professional hit by outfielder Connie Heard, who became the Nashua Dodgers' fifth black ballplayer, following Campanella, Newcombe, Bankhead and Ramon Rodriguez, the Cuban. Heard was signed by Brooklyn scout Bob Tarleton, who discovered him playing semi-pro ball in his hometown of Texas City, Texas, about 35 miles southeast of Houston.

Heard actually made his Dodgers debut the night before, starting in left field and reaching base four times despite being hitless in a doubleheader sweep of Springfield. Heard was, however, at the center of a controversial play at second base in the second game which resulted in a near riot at Holman Stadium.

With Heard on first base in the eighth inning, Billy Hunter dropped a bunt that Cubs first baseman James Forbes fielded and threw to second baseman Lou Macrinotis. Umpire John Bola called Heard out, even though Macrinotis was neither on the bag nor seemed to tag Heard.

Mulleavy tore out of the Dodgers' dugout in a rage to confront Bola and was ejected nearly immediately. The scene became so threatening that police were dispatched to Holman Stadium to monitor the crowd. After the doubleheader, Bola and crewmate Jiggs Donahue were placed in a police cruiser to be ushered away from the stadium and out of harm's way.

Bola returned for his car the next day and found his tires slashed.

For Heard, it was quite a debut, and most certainly had to be the highlight of his stay in Nashua. On July 28, the speedy outfielder was given his outright release not long after singling as a pinch hitter in the ninth inning of the Dodgers' 12–1 loss to Pawtucket. Heard hit just .200 with 1 RBI in 10 games.

Belardi went 3-for-6 and scored two runs in the Dodgers' doubleheader sweep of the Slaters in Pawtucket on July 14, his final games with the Dodgers.

His Dodgers teammates gave Belardi a rousing sendoff, regaling him with a goodbye song on the bus ride north from Pawtucket to a Boston hotel, where he stayed before leaving the next morning for Greenville. Belardi was in tears when his teammates escorted him into the hotel lobby and said to Mulleavy, "Gee, I hate to leave Nashua."

Belardi played parts of four seasons with Brooklyn before moving on to the Tigers for two-plus seasons.

He wouldn't be the last prospect to leave, however. Three days later, pitcher Marion Fricano and outfielder Don Taylor were promoted to Single-A Pueblo of the Western League. Fricano finished his Nashua career with an 11–3 record, including two shutouts, and would end up leading the New England League with a minuscule 1.48 ERA. He would spend four seasons in the majors with the Athletics.

Taylor hit .263 with 15 doubles, one triple, one homer and 39 RBIs.

"Everyone knew what was happening. The Dodgers knew they weren't going to have a team there next year, so they started sending players everywhere," Billy Hunter said.

It was discouraging for the players, who despite the wholesale turnover were still clinging to first place in the New England League, 3½ games ahead of Pawtucket. But it was reaching the point where the fun had been removed. Baseball had become a business.

"We used to pray for rain so we could go into Boston," Kehoe remembered. "Murphy knew all the nightclubs in Boston. It was a good escape for us."

◆ ◆ ◆ ◆

The headline stretching across the top of the front page of the July 13 *Nashua Telegraph* shouldn't have come as a shock to anyone:

N.E. League May Be Four Team Circuit
Fall River, Lynn and Manchester Ready to Quit

With Providence already gone, and Fall River, Lynn and Manchester losing large amounts of money, only Nashua, Pawtucket, Springfield and Portland, the four teams in the league with major league affiliations—and thousands of dollars of money infused to keep them afloat—held any hopes of continuing.

An emergency meeting of league representatives was scheduled for July 15 in Boston, but despite the dire circumstances, representatives of the Manchester, Lynn and Fall River franchises again initially decided to continue their participation. Three days later, though, on July 18, Manchester withdrew from the league. Fall River and Lynn followed the next day. Their players were declared free agents, free to sign with any of the remaining New England League teams.

Eberly's four-team schedule, which would allow Nashua, Pawtucket, Providence and Springfield to finish the season, was put into effect on July 20 with the official start of the second half of the season. At season's end, the three teams with the best second-half record would advance to the playoffs, a revision of Eberly's previous plan. A semifinal series would determine which two teams would meet in a seven-game championship series.

The lead story on the front page of the July 19 edition of *The Nashua Telegraph* made it clear to Nashua baseball fans that Brooklyn was obviously placing the onus of the Nashua Dodgers' future squarely on their shoulders.

Brooklyn to Keep Nashua Club Operating –
Attendance to Determine Plan for Next Year

Dodgers officials most certainly had noticed that even the Manchester Yankees, who had fielded an awful team and pulled the plug after compiling a 28–44 record, had still managed to outdraw their downriver rivals.

"The Dodgers have agreed to give Nashua fans a final chance to show whether they are willing to support a Class B team in minor league baseball or not, even though the (financial) losses for the first half of the season have been rather commanding," Stawasz wrote.

Nashua had taken a four-game winning streak and first-place standing into a game against Springfield, Stawasz noted, and hardly more than a couple hundred fans showed up at Holman. Few of the Dodgers' crowds had surpassed 1,000.

Certainly the economic situation had had some effect on admissions, "but even at its worst, the situation has never warranted such diligent negligence of the Dodgers by the fans, especially in view of the fact that Branch Rickey Sr. has assembled here one of the finest Class B teams in the business," Stawasz wrote.

Many baseball insiders felt the NEL took a huge risk at the beginning of the season by allowing some of its teams to continue despite not being on firm financial footing. *The Sporting News* reported that the New England League and the six-team Class B Colonial League, which was also suffering financially, were rumored to be considering pooling resources to form a new league in 1950.

League representatives, however, were more concerned with completing the 1949 season first without any further disruptions.

On July 19, the Dodgers' 10–5 victory over Fall River in the first-half finale—and the Indians' final professional baseball game in the NEL—gave Nashua a 53–22 record, an outstanding .707 winning percentage and a 2½-game edge over second-place Pawtucket in the final standings. It was a victory Dodgers players and their fans would have cherished had they known how scant wins would be in the second half.

◆ ◆ ◆ ◆

To make up for the losses of Loes, Cimoli, Belardi, Fricano and Taylor, Nashua added outfielders Heard, Zaben "Arky" Arakelian of Haverhill, Mass., and George Boston, who had played for the 1948 squad, as well as first baseman Bob Mitchell, and pitchers Bob Austin, Dick Lovell and Lowell Grosskopf.

Nashua dropped the final three games of a four-game series at Springfield before returning home to play in front of just over 200 fans at Holman. Nob Habel pitched a seven-hitter as Nashua edged Pawtucket, 4–3.

The next night, Pawtucket outfielder Bob Montag put a cap on one of the best games of the year when his 440-foot homer off Bill Mosser in the top of the 12th was the only run in the Slaters' 1–0 victory. Dick Carmichael threw a four-hitter to get the win for Pawtucket, which only managed six hits off Mosser through the first 10 innings.

"I remember that game," Mosser said. "I was pitching really well through the first 11 innings and I made one mistake and Montag crushed it.

"That was probably one of the best games I ever pitched."

Montag, who weeks earlier had had his 18-game hitting streak snapped, made a lot of pitchers pay for their mistakes in 1949. He was unquestionably the league's best hitter. By season's end, his numbers were staggering, and surely had to be one of the best seasons in the long and storied history of the many incarnations of the New England League: .423 batting average, 192 hits, 36 doubles, 18 triples, 21 homers, 43 stolen bases, 91 runs batted in. He had a .720 slugging percentage and his walk-to-strikeout ratio was better than 2-to-1 (116–51). All this in only 125 games.

Montag's homer was the catalyst for the Dodgers' freefall of five straight losses to the Slaters, a streak that also included the loss of shortstop Billy Hunter, who was taken off the field on a stretcher with a sprained back after a takeout slide by Pawtucket's 6-foot-2, 210-pound first baseman, George Crowe.

Crowe, the first black player signed by the Boston Braves, who also played professional basketball with Jackie Robinson with the Los Angeles Devils in 1946, would hit .354 in the NEL in 1949 and made it to the majors with the Braves in 1952, becoming a pinch-hitter extraordinaire over a nine-year career.

Arakelian's career in Nashua lasted seven games and the team finally released the .148-hitting outfielder after he misjudged two fly balls that dropped in for three Pawtucket runs and extended the Dodgers' losing streak.

A few days later, Lovell was optioned to Hazelton (Pa.) of the Class D North Atlantic League after giving up seven hits and 10 walks in nine innings with a 9.00 ERA.

Twelve games into the second half, Nashua was already five games behind first-place Pawtucket. To make matters worse, the injury woes continued when second baseman Bobby Brown badly sprained his ankle on a slide in the third inning of a game against Portland. He was placed on the disabled list and returned to his South Dayton, N.Y., home to recuperate, not returning to the lineup for three weeks.

One of the few highlights of the week came when infielder Bobby Crain was married to local girl Judith A. Chapman at the First Baptist Church in Nashua, with backup catcher Rudy Antonetz serving as his best man.

The Dodgers, in a last-ditch effort to bolster the shoddy attendance numbers in the midst of playing their worst baseball of the season, decided on Aug. 7 to drop the admission price from 80 cents to 65 cents for a homestand against Springfield.

"A number of persons have said that if admission prices were lower, they would attend the games," Eberly said. "We are going to lower the admissions scale and try to see if that is the reason for our drop in attendance."

If attendance did pick up, Eberly planned to keep the admission price at the new lower level.

But Eberly soon realized that lower ticket prices wouldn't translate into more success at the box office. A disappointing crowd—outnumbered by those who decided to attend a free concert by the American Legion band in Greeley Park—saw the Dodgers kick off the homestand with a 5–1 win over Springfield.

After splitting the four-game series against the Cubs and getting swept in a three-game series at Springfield, the Dodgers were 8–18, eight games out of first place and sputtering toward the end. With three weeks left in the regular season, it was clear that the Dodgers would miss the playoffs for the first time in four years. It was also becoming increasingly clear that baseball fans in Nashua had a better chance of building a snowman on Library Hill on Independence Day than seeing the Dodgers playing in Holman Stadium next season.

❖ ❖ ❖ ❖

Whatever doubt remained regarding the future of the Nashua Dodgers in the eyes of baseball fans and city business leaders, Bill Eberly was crystal clear on what lay ahead.

"By the middle of August, I knew the Dodgers would be leaving Nashua," Eberly said. "I received a call from Brooklyn to pack all of the office equipment, uniforms, etc., and ship it to Ebbets Field after the last game.

"There was a terrible feeling that I had failed, despite the fact that we had four major league prospects and had won 53 games in the first half of the season. There wasn't much interest in my Nashua Dodgers. Even those well-planned promotions and the good weather in July and August hadn't helped attendance."

On Aug. 26, the dismantling of the Dodgers continued. Hunter, who hit just .235 in 95 games but was an anchor at shortstop, was shipped to Class A Newport News, Va. Hunter would reach the major leagues in 1953 and be chosen an All-Star as a rookie with the St. Louis Browns.

A flashy fielder, Hunter spent six seasons in the majors and finished with a career .219 batting average in 630 games. He was the Baltimore Orioles' third-base coach from 1975–77 and managed the Texas Rangers to a 146–108 record in 1977 and '78.

As badly as Nashua played in the second half of the season, the Dodgers remained alive in the playoff race until being swept by Springfield in a doubleheader at Holman Stadium on Sept. 4. Nashua lost three of its final five games, but closed out the season with a 6–0 win over the Cubs before 600 fans—43 fewer than the team's per-game average for the season—in the second game of a Labor Day doubleheader at Holman Stadium. Norm Postolese, who hit .280 over 117 games and was the only Dodgers outfielder to stay with the team for the entire season, belted his only homer of the season in the finale.

Antonetz, who finished with a .225 average in 73 games, went 5-for-5 in the last game while Al Gilbert threw a complete-game five-hitter.

The day before, J.J. Murphy was presented with a three-way portable radio after being voted the most popular Dodger by the fans. It was the only presentation on a day that in years past had been a rather elaborate celebration of the season.

The season-ending victory dropped the curtain "on the Gate City's final professional showing for, perhaps, many years to come," wrote Stawasz, whose prophecy proved true: Nashua did not get another professional baseball franchise until 1983 when the California Angels' Eastern League franchise took up residence at Holman.

"Slightly more than 600 paid admissions watched the Dodgers die . . ." Stawasz wrote in *The Nashua Telegraph* two days after the final game. "Yup, brother, that was the end of our New England League Dodgers. You can blame it on television, bad times, indifference or simply a matter of reaching the financial saturation point. Whatever the reason, it spells '*finis*,' with all capital letters to boot.

"(The return of baseball) came to us after a long sleep. . . . We shall sleep again, baseball-wise, perhaps forever."

From 1946–51, minor league baseball enjoyed what many considered its golden age. In 1945, only about a dozen leagues existed across the country. One year later, there were 41, a nearly 350 percent increase in operating leagues. Ironically, the minors' best year was 1949, when 59 leagues were represented in 438 cities.

In 1950, minor league baseball received a huge jolt when

its attendance fell by more than seven million. The downward spiral continued as the United States entered the Korean War. A total of 43 leagues started the 1952 season; but by 1956 there were only 27 leagues in operation. Twenty-one remained in 1959.

The face of baseball had changed, and, for many fans in the country's smaller towns and cities, the heady days of hometown pride in the local nine were gone forever.

On Sept. 18, 1949, Portland scored eight runs in the first inning and went on to crush Springfield, 11–0, to win the Governor's Cup finals, four games to two.

The Portland Pilots were champions of a league that had drawn its last breath.

◆ ◆ ◆ ◆

Outside *The Nashua Telegraph*'s Main Street offices on Oct. 5, dozens of baseball fans gathered to watch a television donated by Jerry's Radio Shop broadcast the first game of the 1949 World Series between the Brooklyn Dodgers and New York Yankees. Just over two hundred miles to the southeast—right there on the grainy black and white screen—favorite son Don Newcombe was staring in for a sign from battery-mate Roy Campanella.

Newcombe, in the final days of a fabulous season that would earn him the Rookie of the Year Award, pitched an outstanding game, giving up just four hits before Dodger killer Tommy Henrich hit a leadoff home run to right in the bottom of the ninth to give the Yankees a 1–0 victory in Game 1.

Newcombe pitched a tremendous game, giving up only five hits while striking out 11 and walking none. His performance was bettered by Yankees starter Allie Reynolds, who gave up just two hits and four walks while striking out nine.

The 23-year-old Newcombe would be tagged with his second loss of the series in Game 4, a 6–4 Yankees win, before New York closed out the series on Oct. 9 with a 10–6 win in Game 5.

Campanella would hit only .267 in the series with one home run and two RBIs.

For the Yankees, the 1949 championship represented the first of five straight—including three against the Dodgers. Brooklyn would finally capture its first World Series title in 1955—beating the Yankees, four games to three. Nashua alumni Newcombe, Campanella. Don Hoak, Billy Loes and their manager, Walter Alston, would all earn World Series rings.

Three years later, the Brooklyn Dodgers and New York Giants shocked the baseball world and headed west, landing in Los Angeles and San Francisco, respectively. Baseball's landscape had been irrevocably altered.

"I'll never forget Nashua's baseball fans," Campanella said in an interview with Stawasz before the start of the 1949 Series. "I have been playing baseball for a dozen years and no city in the United States was a nicer place to live than in your town. I'd like to go back some day."

Roy Campanella never did make it back to Nashua. Some would say neither did baseball.

Afterword

THERE WAS LOTS OF GOOD news about the 1949 Nashua Dodgers season. We had four major league prospects in first baseman Wayne Belardi, pitcher Billy Loes, right fielder Gino Cimoli and shortstop Billy Hunter. And we won plenty of games early in the season with what I thought was the best team in the league.

But by July the bad news began to dominate the league and the Nashua Dodgers.

Attendance declined dramatically at Holman Stadium and we didn't draw flies at most of the other ballparks in the league. Providence, Fall River, Lynn and Manchester didn't finish the season.

I got in hot water with Fred Dobens, the editor of *The Nashua Telegraph* about remarks I had made regarding Nashua's poor attendance and at other New England cities because of the collapse of the textile industry. And the Chamber of Commerce wasn't too happy with my comments about the status of Nashua's economic condition, either.

By the middle of August I knew that the Dodgers would be leaving Nashua. There was a terrible feeling that I had failed, despite the fact we had those prospects and we won 71 games.

In September 1949, I had this terrible worry about my future with the Dodgers, even the future of the national pastime. I was young and wanted very much to be successful in the baseball business. I wondered if my failures in Nashua would end my dream of someday making it to the major leagues. I got there, leaving Brooklyn in 1954 to become business manager of the Milwaukee Braves for 11 years.

But I can't help wonder what might have been in Nashua.

Bill Eberly
Nashua Dodgers Business Manager (1948–49)
Dec. 12, 1999

Bibliography

Alston, Walter, and Burick, Si, *Alston and the Dodgers* (Doubleday & Co. 1966).

Campanella, Roy, *It's Good To Be Alive* (University of Nebraska Press, 1995).

Clark, Dick and Lester, Larry, *The Negro Leagues Book* (The Society of American Baseball Research, 1994).

Johnson, Lloyd and Wolff, Miles, *The Encyclopedia of Minor League Baseball, 2nd edition* (Baseball America, 1997).

Kahn, Roger, *The Boys of Summer* (Perennial Library, 1987, Harper & Row, 1972).

Moffi, Larry and Kronstadt, Jonathan, *Crossing the Line: Black Major Leaguers 1947–1959* (University of Iowa Press, 1994).

Peterson, Robert, *Only The Ball Was White* (Oxford University Press, 1970).

Robinson, Rachel (with Lee Daniels), *Jackie Robinson: An Intimate Portrait* (Abrams, 1996)

Shatkin, Mike and Charlton, Jim, *The Ballplayers* (William Morrow and Company, 1990).

Shepard, Florence Crosby and Lawrence, Brian, *Nashua, New Hampshire: A Pictorial History* (The Donning Company Publishers, 1989).

The Baseball Encyclopedia, 10th edition (MacMillan Books, 1996).

The Nashua Experience: History in the Making (Phoenix Publishing, 1978).

The Nashua Telegraph, Dec. 1946–Dec. 1949 editions.

Tygiel, Jules, *Baseball's Great Experiment: Jackie Robinson and His Legacy* (Oxford University Press, 1997).

NASHUA DODGERS
FROM A to Z

A

Walter "Walt" Abplanalp, pitcher (1948)
Andrew "Doc" Alexopoulos (Alexson), first baseman (1948)
Walter Alston, first baseman/manager (1946)
Rudolph "Rudy" Antonetz, catcher (1949)
Zaben "Arky" Arakelian, outfielder (1949)
Robert "Bob" Austin, pitcher (1949)

B

Daniel "Dan" Bankhead, pitcher (1948)
Ted Barczuk (Bartz), outfielder/third baseman (1948)
E.J. "Buzzie" Bavasi, business manager (1946)
Wayne Belardi, first baseman (1949)
Chester "Chet" Beres, pitcher (1948)
Charles "Charlie" Bird, pitcher (1948)
Joseph "Joe" Bodan, outfielder (1946–47)
Jean Bournot, pitcher (1947)

George Boston, outfielder (1948–49)
William Braam, pitcher (1948)
George Brown, pitcher (1946)
Robert "Bobby" Brown, second baseman/outfielder (1949)

C
Roy "Campy" Campanella, catcher (1946)
Alexander "Al" Campanis, second baseman/manager (1948)
Philip "Flip" Cardinale, outfielder (1948)
John Carey, manager (1947)
Donald Chartier, pitcher (1946)
Gino Cimoli, outfielder (1949)
Alden Clark, business manager (1947)
Robert "Bobby" Crain, shortstop/third baseman (1949)

D
William "Billy DeMars, shortstop (1946)
Richard "Dick" Detzel, outfielder (1946)
Otis Davis, outfielder (1947)
Jerry Dolan, pitcher (1948)

E
William "Bill" Eberly, business manager (1948–49)

F
Marion Fricano, pitcher (1947, 1949)

G
Oscar "Gus" Galipeau, catcher/first baseman (1946–47)
Alton "Al" Gilbert, pitcher (1949)

Peter "Pete" Giordano, pitcher (1947–48)
Norm "Goose" Gosselin, pitcher (1949)
Leon Griffeth, pitcher (1948)
Lowell Grosskopf, pitcher (1949)
Fred Gutherz, shortstop (1948)

H
Norbert "Nob" Habel, pitcher (1949)
Connie Heard, outfielder (1949)
Donald Hilbert, outfielder (1949)
Donald "Don" Hoak, shortstop/third baseman (1948)
Dan Horne, pitcher (1947)
Gordon "Billy" Hunter, shortstop (1949)

K
William "Bill" Kalbaugh, outfielder (1946)
William "Bill" Kean, pitcher (1949)
William "Bill" Kearns, shortstop (1948)
Robert "Bob" Kehoe, third baseman/shortstop (1949)
Robert "Bobby Kellogg, outfielder/first baseman/second
    baseman/third baseman (1946–47)
Michael "Mike" King, shortstop (1947)
Walter King, shortstop (1947)
Peter "Moose" Kousagan, outfielder (1948)

L
Gerald Laplante, outfielder (1949)
Robert E. "Bob" Lee, outfielder (1948)
Stanley "Stan" Lipka, third baseman/shortstop/first baseman
    (1946–47)

William "Billy" Loes, pitcher (1949)
Richard Lovell, pitcher (1949)
Robert "Bobby" Ludwick, pitcher (1947–49)

M
Louis "Lou" Magee, shortstop (1948)
James Massar, shortstop (1947)
Merrill McDonald, first baseman (1949)
James "Jim" McFadden, pitcher (1946)
Lorne McNeeley, third baseman (1949)
Robert "Bob" Milliken, pitcher (1947)
Robert D. "Bob" Mitchell, first baseman (1949)
Richard "Dick" Mlady, pitcher (1946)
Karl Morrison, pitcher (1948)
William "Bill" Mosser, pitcher (1949)
John "J.J." Murphy, catcher (1948–49)

N
Russell Nelson, second baseman (1948)
Donald "Don" Newcombe, pitcher (1946–47)
Peter Nicolis, pitcher (1949)
Michael "Mike" Nozinski, pitcher (1946)

O
Robert Oley, pitcher (1948)
Francis "Frank" O'Neil, catcher (1948)
Paul O'Neil, catcher (1947)
Joseph "Joe" O'Neill, pitcher (1946)

P

Glen Page, pitcher (1948)

Henry "Harry" Parker, third baseman/second
    baseman/left fielder (1948)

Harvey Porter, outfielder (1946)

Norman "Norm" Postolese, outfielder (1949)

Q

Maurice "Mike" Quill, pitcher (1948)

R

Alfred Rehm, shortstop (1946)

Bernard "Bernie" Reinertsen, pitcher (1946–47)

Joseph "Joe" Rioli, outfielder (1949)

Gordon Roach, pitcher (1949)

Ramon Rodriguez, catcher (1947)

Walter Rogers, third baseman/shortstop (1947–48)

James "Jim" Romano, pitcher (1947)

Louis "Lou" Ruchser, first baseman (1947)

Francis "Frank" Ruminski, pitcher (1946–47)

S

James Salada, catcher (1948)

William "Bill" Samson, pitcher (1948–49)

Michael "Mike" Santora, pitcher (1947)

Lawrence "Larry" Shepard, pitcher (1946)

Anthony "Tony" Sierzega, pitcher (1948–49)

Francis Smith, pitcher (1947)

Henry Smith, pitcher (1948)
Joseph "Joe" Soskovic, catcher (1948)
George Souza, pitcher (1947)
Samuel Sporn, outfielder (1947)
Robert Sundstrom, pitcher (1948)

T
Donald "Don" Taylor, outfielder (1949)
Alan Thomaier, outfielder (1948)
Joseph "Joe" Tuminelli, second baseman/third baseman (1946)

V
Clayton Van Cott, pitcher (1946–47)
Robert "Bob" Vickery, pitcher/manager (1947)

W
James Walsh, pitcher (1948)
Jack Wernert, pitcher (1946)
Charles "Dean" Wood, second baseman (1946–47)
Aaron "Bubbles" Weisenberg, pitcher (1947)

Y
Edward "Eddie" Yaeger, outfielder (1946–47, 1949)

Z
Joseph "Joe" Zack, outfielder (1949)
Francis "Fran" Zeisz, pitcher (1948)

About the Author

STEVE DALY is the assistant sports editor of *The Telegraph* of Nashua, New Hampshire. A 1988 graduate of Northeastern University, Daly joined *The Telegraph* in 1989 as a sports reporter before becoming assistant sports editor in 1994. In 1997, Daly was awarded first place by the New England Press Association for Coverage of a Racial or Ethnic Issue.

He has also worked for *The Sun* of Lowell, Massachusetts, and *The Portsmouth (N.H.) Herald.*

Daly resides in Lowell, Massachusetts, with his wife, Maureen, and daughters, Brooke and Katherine.